A
Postcard
to
Heaven

A
Postcard
to
Heaven

by
Duane Parrish

New Leaf Press

Library of Congress Catalog Number: 93-84140
ISBN: 0-89221-235-7

Cover design by: Farewell Communications

Dedication

This book is dedicated to my family, without whose help I could not have made it through the trial:

My wife, Violet, who stood by my side and refused to let me wallow in self-pity. She believed in me!

My son Mark, who at the very onset said, "Dad, let's pray," and he did.

My daughter Patrece, who was so patient and understanding.

My father and mother, who taught me the ways of God at an early age.

Without these people I wouldn't be what I am today.

P O S T C A R D S

Preface

In a world that is filled with so much pain, heartache, and trouble, I would like to think that I could share with the reader some lessons that took me from the abyss of despair into the ocean of God's enormous grace and infinite love.

The story is told of a visitor who went to a famous potter to observe the art of molding a vessel. He watched as the potter beat a lump of clay with a large mallet. It looked as if nothing was happening, and the man said to the potter, "Sir, why are you doing that?"

He replied, "Just wait and watch the results — then you will understand."

The man heeded the advice and soon noted that the top of the mass of clay began to quiver and swell as little bumps formed on its surface.

"Now you can see the need for the pounding," said the potter. "I could never shape the clay into a worthwhile vessel if these bubbles remained in the clay. So I must gradually work them out."

I found myself on God's potter's wheel in 1980. As He began to start the molding process, I felt the mallet of God come down on me and I saw more clearly than ever before why the great Potter must work on the souls of those He loves.

The discipline of chastening, testing, and trials God allowed me to go through was necessary to eliminate pride and self-will from my life

I found the picture of myself in Jeremiah 18, where Jeremiah was told to go to the potter's house.

"So I went down to the potter's house, and I saw him working at the wheel. But the pot he was shaping from the clay was marred in his hands; so the potter formed it into another pot, shaping it as seemed best to him" (Jer. 18:3-4;NIV).

In the early days of my recovery I didn't like what was going on, but the more I submitted to the Master Potter, the more peace and joy I found, and it continues today.

It is my sincere desire that as you read this book you will experience the grace and the love of God that was shown to me in my deepest despair, and that you will allow God to mold you into the vessel which will glorify Him.

P O S T C A R D
O N E

Out of My Darkness

Desperate, I clutched the .30-caliber Magnum pistol in my fist as I searched my office for a bullet to end my ministry and my life.

Beside me, my wife screamed and pleaded, grabbing at my hand. I pushed her away.

In answer to a dark and seducing altar call, I sought to end my personal nightmare. Resolved no longer to linger and walk this terrible aisle alone, I decided the time had come to put an end to this tiring, unfulfilling testimony my life had become.

Despite the prayers of hundreds of loving people, I had not been healed. Despite their faith, I was not restored.

Regardless of their patient support and my own attempts to lean on Jesus, I had become a shadow of the preacher I once had been.

And now that dark afternoon, I'd had enough. In my weakness, as Violet wept, I frantically rummaged through my closet for a single round of ammunition. All I needed was one bullet to let me bring down this torment, destroy this temple, and silence forever the sound of my loved one's anguished cries.

Distressed that I had shoved her, Violet bowed her head and wept, stunned by my rejection. In my misery and anger, as I searched for just a single bullet, I heard her slump to the floor beside the living room couch. In desperation, she began to intercede aloud in prayer, her voice full of grief.

She poured out her heart to God on my behalf.

She was so tired. This was not fair to her. I just wanted the torment and frustration to end. It had been six months of constant battle.

So many times it seemed, my most valiant efforts were met with people trying to complete my sentences. My speech was still slurred and inappropriate words were still slipping from my embarrassed lips. Although I would try my best, I saw the averted eyes while people waited seemingly forever as I finished what I had to say.

Almost 200 long days had passed since I had come home from emergency brain surgery — since the long hours that our congregation had knelt in intercession for my recovery. For weeks members had brought in meals for my darling little girl, my faithful teenage son, and my devoted, dedicated, determined wife.

Now, long after so many who loved me and believed in me had grown weary of my lingering handicaps, here I was — still struggling. All of us had been ready long ago for me to be completely well, a marvelous testimony to God's healing power.

But after months of therapy and rehabilitation, I could still only say a few words like "car" or "bike" — just one-syllable words with no controlled inflection in my voice at all. Many times my words were badly garbled.

I could not read. I could not write. I could not spell. Progress was excruciatingly slow.

It had become so discouraging. That afternoon, Violet and I had been on our way to see an inspirational movie — the story of Joni, the Christian woman who suffered such terrible handicaps yet lived to praise God. My associate pastor, Greg Hickman, and his wife picked us up.

As we were driving over together, I kept trying to communicate with Greg, but he just could not understand me. He kept saying, "I don't understand, Pastor. What is it you are trying to say?"

I must have repeated it four or five times, and he finally said, "I think you are trying to say 'I don't like to be born'?"

What I was trying to say was, "I curse the day that I was born." This gives you an idea of how hard it was for me to communicate.

You can also see how low I was that afternoon.

Battling the depression that lurked around every corner became harder every day. I was growing weary of trying so very hard. Finally, I had given in, allowing myself to wallow in self-pity.

As the film was about to start, the Holy Spirit began to deal with me. Deep within, I sensed the question: What sermons have you preached to your people that have meant the most to you?

Immediately I recalled two. One was on praise and worship. As the movie began, I kept going back over and over what I had preached: You have got to praise God for who He is not for what He can do for you.

I don't know why that thought stuck in my mind. I had delivered that sermon before any symptoms of my illness had developed. As I sat there thinking about that message, I was convicted.

I had praised God for the good things that happened to me, such as my kids' good grades, my wife's beautiful singing, the church board giving us a raise in salary, or for good attendance in church.

But very rarely had I gone out and looked up into the sky and said, "God, have I told You lately how much I love You? You are awesome. To think that You would abide with me and have communication with me. I just love You for that."

Then the second sermon I'd preached came to mind. It was on the sovereignty of God. As the plot of the movie screen unfolded, my mind was on that sermon. I remembered one line I had preached: It's God's ball game, and He's got a right to call the shots in our lives, knowing this one thing: He always does it for our good, not for our demise. Thus, we have Romans 8:28, and we know that all things work together for good.

For a moment, I considered the supremacy and majesty of the Almighty.

Up on the movie screen, Joni dove off into the shallow lake water and broke her neck. The ambulance rushed her to the hospital. Suddenly, the gurney was pictured crashing through the emergency room doors.

At that moment, the Lord quickened in me this

question, If I don't heal you past this present stage, will you still praise Me?

I got very angry. What a rotten thing to ask of me. How could a loving God ask that?

I reacted in a flash of anger and desperation, *No, no, no! I mean, come on, You've got to be kidding. This is all the thanks I get for serving You from the age of five and preaching since I was sixteen? No, thank You!*

I grew so angry that I cried through most of the movie. Violet sensed something was wrong but did not know what it was. I shrugged off her quiet inquiries and offered no explanation. How could I convey my agony over such concepts when my vocabulary had been reduced to single words? Did anybody even believe that I was still capable of any such deep thoughts?

I blocked her out and suffered alone.

Miserably, I kept to myself the rest of that afternoon, morosely ignoring everybody, wallowing in my anger and self-pity.

When we got home, I went straight into my study. Violet followed me — upset, concerned, and determined not to let me out of her sight.

I shoved her away and went to the closet where I kept my .30-caliber Magnum pistol. I searched for a bullet to load into the chamber — intent on my own suicide.

In the living room, Violet prayed, interceding without mincing any words, "God, I can't stop Duane, but we need Your help. Help us, please."

I was cut to my deepest core and immediately convicted of my self-pity.

She had been there for me day upon unending day, and now I had shown my appreciation by shoving her away. I had shown my gratitude by rejecting her.

I stared at my gun.
I dropped it to the floor.
I wept.
Today I refer to that afternoon as the beginning of the rest of my life.

Little Barroom Preacher

My Christian life began at a very early age.

Up until I was five years old, I didn't think I needed to get saved because my dad was a pastor. I figured that assured my salvation.

I don't remember discussing this flawed theology with my father, but I am sure he would have been aghast. But five year olds don't pay all that much attention to sermons — even if their daddy is in the pulpit.

Then, a traveling husband-wife evangelistic team came through and held a two-week revival at our church. They took turns preaching.

One night the wife — whose name was Mildred

Byers — told us, "God has no grandchildren."

I immediately understood. She was saying that I couldn't get into heaven just because my dad was a preacher.

I was stunned.

Here I was already in kindergarten, and I had done nothing to personally accept Jesus into my heart.

I realized I wanted to get saved — before it was too late. After all, if Jesus came that night, I didn't want to be the only one in my family left behind.

Years later, I would read a renowned essay by the late David du Plessis that makes the very same point as the lady preacher: that God has no grandkids; He only has sons and daughters.

It didn't make any difference if my dad was a pastor, or a member of the board of directors of our denomination, or even the greatest evangelist ever to live — I still had to get right with my Maker.

As she closed her sermon, Mrs. Byers asked those who wanted to repent of their sins to come forward. I found myself walking the aisle, joining the others who had lifted their hands for salvation.

I told Mrs. Byers, "I want to get saved."

She knelt with me and said, "Now, I want you to repent of all your sins."

What sins? I asked myself. *I haven't been drunk, I haven't dipped snuff, and I haven't done any running around with wild women.* Then I thought, *Uh-oh. I know.*

My dad had told me not to say any sugar-coated swear words. He had sat me down and said, "So you will understand, this is what I am talking about. Don't say heck, gee whiz, gosh, by golly ..." and he went through all the words.

He said, "If I hear you saying those, I will wash your mouth out with soap."

So when he left that day, I went into an empty Sunday school classroom, and I said, "Heck. Heck. Heck. Heck. Heck."

I did it in rebellion to my dad.

So that was my confession of sin. I confessed to God, "I'm sorry for being rebellious and for saying 'heck' all those times. Forgive me, God, and come into my heart."

You may scoff about the spiritual depth of a kindergartner, but I want you to know that my conversion that night was real.

Furthermore, I wanted to share my faith with the unsaved. I didn't want to share it with Christian people; I wanted to share it with rank sinners.

I couldn't read yet, but we had a children's church teacher who had taught us all sorts of memory verses. So I took my little New Testament — the one put out by the Gideons — and I asked myself, *Where can I share?*

On Main Street, down from my father's church, there were six taverns. I had heard about the sin and degradation that went on in those dens of iniquity. So I marched into the nearest tavern and announced in my high, little-boy voice, "Listen up, guys, if you don't get right with God, you're going to hell."

Every beer stein froze. The bartender stared — stunned, motionless. Twenty faces looked around to see who was talking — but they couldn't see me because I was shorter than the table at the front door.

But when they all stood, they gawked down in amazement at me peering up at them in righteous judgment. I clutched my Gideon's New Testament and struck what I believed to be a proper preacherly pose — with one finger in the air and my Bible clutched to my heart.

Now I had their attention.

Nobody said a word. They were absolutely dumbfounded. I took that as my cue.

Since my dad always would tell his congregation to "Turn to such-and-such in your Bible," I figured I should, too.

Just like he always did, I licked my finger and shuffled some pages and told them to turn to John 3:16. I turned four or five pages, but since I couldn't read, I probably turned to the table of contents or the begats. I don't know where I was, but I pointed my finger to the page and said, "For God so loved the world, that he gave his only begotten Son, that whosoever believeth in him should not perish, but have everlasting life."

Then I said, "Secondly," and I held up two fingers, "you're going to hell because my father says so, and he's a preacher."

One guy on a barstool snarled, "Shut that kid up."

A guy next to him said, "You leave that kid alone because what he is saying is the truth."

And right there before my astonished eyes, the first guy pulled a knife. He lunged right at me — he was actually that furious.

The second guy yelled at me to run and then threw himself onto my attacker.

I started to run, but first I looked back and saw blood coming from the neck of my rescuer.

I was breathless by the time I got home.

I had taken the gospel to the very gates of hell — and the demons had fought back!

I didn't dare tell my dad about my adventure.

Years later, I was holding a meeting in Grants Pass, Oregon, and the Holy Spirit brought this story to my mind. I was preaching about how each of us has a purpose, even little children. I preached that our purpose is to win souls for the Master, and I used my adventure to illustrate my point. I said, "I planted the seed. I don't know what happened next, but I planted the seed."

After the altar call, an older guy came up to me, grinning like a Cheshire cat, and he said, "Do you remember me?"

I said, "I don't think I have ever seen you before."

He said, "See this scar on my neck? I was the guy who saved your life that day in the bar. I've been praying that God would lead me across your path someday so I could thank you. Since then, I have become a Christian. I'm a pastor at a neighboring town here, and I just want to thank you for sharing your faith."

Now, I was the one who was dumbfounded.

Looking back on my first sermon, I don't think it would have won any prizes in a theological contest, but it was certainly shared with enthusiasm. And it bore fruit, even though I was only five years old.

I wish I could tell you that I stayed on the straight-and-narrow road for the rest of my childhood. The truth is that I went the way of many preacher's sons and spent a semi-rebellious period almost disgracing my father.

When I was about 13 years old, I was going along with what other junior high schoolers were wearing at the time. In fact, I looked like one of those James Dean posters you see in 1950s nostalgia restaurants — or like Fonzie on the old Happy Days television show.

With my hair in a ducktail, I shuffled like a tough guy and had ambitions of being a rock 'n' roll star like

Buddy Holly or Elvis Presley or the Big Bopper.

I even entered a talent contest at school. First prize was a $100 savings bond. In 1957, that was a lot of money. You could buy an old jalopy for $100.

I wanted to win. I had plans for that bond, so I entered the contest.

My dad said, "I think you should sing 'It Is No Secret.'"

"You've got to be kidding, Dad," I scoffed. "That's a church song. I'm going to sing 'Birth of the Blues.'"

So I worked up that number and sure enough I came in first place. Ironically, the second-place prize went to somebody who sang 'It Is No Secret.'

I would walk down the street and people would say, "Oh, that's the cool kid who won the $100 savings bond. Isn't he neat?"

I was somebody!

Well, my dad came into my bedroom one Saturday morning, woke me up, and said, "Duane, here's a dollar. I want you to go get a haircut."

"I don't think I need a haircut," I told him, self-consciously touching my ducktail.

"I don't care what you think you need," responded my father. "I just told you to get a haircut."

Now I don't know what got into me because I was maybe five feet tall and not yet 100 pounds. My dad, on the other hand, was 6-foot-2 and weighed about 225 pounds. I jumped out of that bed and put my hands on my hips and said, "If you think you're man enough to make me, come on and try."

He looked at me with an unamused twinkle in his eyes and set about to show me what happens when a punk picks a fight with a man.

He did his best not to hurt me while knocking me around — just enough to show me that he meant business. It was basically as if a grizzly had been challenged by a cub. However, I guess it sounded like a riot because I remember my mother running into my doorway and exclaiming, "Roland, you're going to kill him."

"I hope I do," my dad roared. "No son is going to talk to me that way and get by with it."

Well, needless to say, my bubble was burst.

I got a haircut.

I also gained a new respect for my dad.

Three years later, when my father sensed that I was hearing the call of God on my life for the ministry, he told me this: "Son, always remember this: The Holy Spirit is a gentleman. He will not cross the threshold of your will."

And so, I entered the ministry at age 16, was licensed as a preacher at age 19, and ordained shortly thereafter.

I gave up the idea of becoming a musical recording artist and decided to be true to my calling — to preach the gospel and sing for Jesus. I formed a singing group, and we began to sing for rallies put on by Youth for Christ. In 1957, we won, in our category, the national contest of Youth for Christ. As a result, we were guests at a big Billy Graham crusade in New York and then went to the World Congress in Denmark.

I had only been home for a few months when an evangelist came through our town and asked my father if I could travel with him. My father felt it would be good for me.

After traveling with him and his wife for three years, I struck out on my own, holding revivals.

After a couple of years, I found myself preaching

an evangelistic crusade in Oceanside, California. In the meetings every night, I saw this very attractive girl. I asked the pastor's wife who she was and learned that she worked for a local supermarket in the cookie bakery.

Suddenly, I developed a craving for cookies of all kinds. We had boxes of cookies in the kitchen, in the bathroom, in the bedrooms — everywhere. The pastor's wife told me I better do something about this craving.

I agreed.

Violet Henson and I fell in love, and in 1962, she became my wife. Married life was wonderful, and we continued to travel and hold crusades, speak at youth camps and in youth conventions.

We had two children, pastored our first church, and traveled three more years before we ended up at Christ Center. This church in Beaverton, Oregon, a suburb of Portland, became our second pastorate. Life was good!

I loved to proclaim God's truth and prayed for his anointing and power. I was delighted with the Lord's call on my life to win souls to Jesus Christ.

As the years passed, I held positions on state church committees as well as the Youth Council. Every summer, I spoke at a lot of youth camps. In addition, I had a daily radio program called "Assembly Lines" on a local station, KPDQ. My ministry was active and fulfilling.

During my tenure, Christ Center had grown from a struggling, discouraged group — that had wanted to merge with another congregation — into a vibrant, effective force in the community. I had a fine associate pastor who was excellent with the youth and was a great man of God.

Believing that the Holy Spirit lived within me, I

preached that "Greater is He that is in me than he that is in the world."

I knew that 2 Timothy 1:7 promises me and all believers that ours is not a spirit of fear, but of power, love, and a sound mind.

As Easter came around, I was showing telltale signs that all was not right, but I honestly didn't think anything was seriously wrong.

It was in the Christ Center pulpit on Easter Sunday that I began a long journey down a dark tunnel into a very personal nightmare.

It was to be a pilgrimage I would not wish upon anyone, but from which I would return with a very real, personal, and powerful understanding of God — and how I am to minister to His hurting people.

Falling Apart

It was Easter morning, 1980.

In accompaniment with our congregation's other musicians, I was playing my saxophone during the worship service. The church was full of visitors all dressed in their Easter finery.

Our special Resurrection Sunday program had been planned carefully, and we all wanted to put our best foot forward. After all, if the only time we are going to see some folks is Easter, then we need to make the service as memorable and stirring as possible.

I did not know it, but my wife had dreamed that something was going to happen to our family. She woke up crying but then couldn't remember what the dream was about.

The next morning she couldn't shake a feeling of

sadness, but one word kept coming to her mind, and she prayed, "God, do You want to say something to me?" The word was "long-suffering," found in Galatians 5:22.

She decided to look the word up in the dictionary and in a biblical commentary I had. The word means "the ability to endure discomfort without fighting back; having patience to see the desired end result come to pass; having the ability to rest and trust in God in the middle of adversity; bearing trouble patiently for a long time."

Violet felt God was preparing her for something.

She couldn't shake that feeling even as the service progressed.

From the platform, I played worshipfully on my soulful sax. As I hit the notes of Bill Gaither's "There's Just Something About That Name," all of a sudden, I couldn't blow air through my mouth.

My palate had collapsed. The medical explanation is something like "myoclonus of the soft palate."

All I know is that suddenly, I could only blow air through my nose — which brought my sax solo to an abrupt halt.

What had happened?

The brain, as I understand it, tells the soft palate, "He is playing the saxophone, and the air has to come out through his mouth," or "He's blowing his nose, the air has to come out through the nose."

However, here I was playing the saxophone and the air was coming out through my nose — and I could do nothing about it.

So I put the sax down and apologized.

My mind was racing. *What's going on? This is not normal.*

Earlier that morning as I had been working on my

sermon, my wife had paused outside of my study. "Why are you scowling so?" she asked.

I looked up, surprised. "How do you spell Jesus?" I asked. "I can't spell Jesus."

Violet squinted at me in concern.

But I thought nothing of it.

However, the bit with the saxophone did get my attention. Something was definitely wrong. I couldn't adequately turn my thoughts into words as I tried to explain to the congregation what had just happened.

So, I just sat down.

Almost immediately, it was time for me to bring the Easter sermon. Well, when I stood, I thought I was okay.

But the minute I opened my mouth, I realized that something was wrong. My mouth could not fit around my thoughts. Common words absolutely evaded me.

I limped through my 20 minutes with long pauses between thoughts. There was a lot of awkward coughing throughout the crowded sanctuary. I tried to ignore it, but I began to feel terrible frustration.

Standing there in the pulpit, I felt the flush of embarrassment as I looked out at the congregation. It was sort of like a bad dream. I wanted to say something clever that would put everybody at ease. Instead, however, I just mumbled something that was nonsensical even to my ears.

Then, I managed to make a coherent statement and went totally blank. I blinked at the congregation and tried to think of what I was talking about.

It was like having the screen on the computer flashing off and on in the middle of typing a letter. In mid-sentence, my mental computer would crash and go dark.

Then I would boot it back up, figure out where I had been, declare some great thought — then go blank again.

It was quite disconcerting.

No one responded to the altar call.

After the final prayer, after I had shaken hands with everybody at the back door, I turned back inside and saw the members of my church board, gathered behind me. There was concern all over their faces.

I tried to be nonchalant, but I was beginning to be worried, too. Something was definitely wrong.

One of the board members cleared his throat, "Pastor," he said slowly, "we think you ought to have a complete medical examination."

I had to admit that I thought so, too.

Violet called a nurse in the congregation who recommended a good doctor.

After a thorough examination — a marathon of 21 different tests — the physician went over the results with me. He said, "Quite frankly, you passed every test. You are in good physical shape."

I said, "Well, what's wrong, doctor? I'm not acting normally."

He felt the tension from pastoring in a metropolitan area was probably getting to me and suggested I get away from the city and relax. "Given your line of work," he said, "I think you're suffering from a nervous collapse."

So, that was it?

I was having a nervous breakdown?

P O S T C A R D
F O U R

Time Off

I went back to my board and said, "Here's what the doctor said — I need some time off. His diagnosis is that I'm suffering from a nervous collapse. I don't know why, but that's what he said."

I did not feel like I'd had any breakdown.

How was I supposed to know what a nervous breakdown feels like? My doctor had credentials, so he should know. The church generously gave me the money we needed for a nice, long vacation.

So, I went back to my study to pick up a few things I thought I would need.

Why me? I asked myself as I puttered around my office, trying to decide what books and notebooks to take with me. *What is God allowing to happen to me?* I asked.

Was He just trying to get my attention? Well, He

certainly had it! Had I been too busy in His work to listen to His voice or seek His will? Had I neglected giving Him my time, my attention, and my affection because of all the plans, goals, and projects that I had undertaken on His behalf?

Was that my sin?

Had I been presumptuous — claiming to do things for God when I was actually doing them for me?

Guilt welled up within me.

Perhaps I was so caught up in my good, godly works — my efforts to help God out — that my scurrying around had choked out the Word of God in my heart and drowned out His voice?

I trembled at the thought. How could I think I could help God out? How could I have been so proud as to think I was doing Him a favor? Was the parable of the sower and the seed in Matthew 13:18-23 aimed at me?

Was my own self-righteous heart the path, the stony soil and the thorns — the places where the seed of the gospel could not prosper? Had I been too busy doing what I had decided was God's will to actually hear Him?

I became convicted that that was the case. I found myself reciting Matthew 11:28-30, where Jesus promises each of us who will come unto Him — we who are overburdened, whose work is too hard, and whose load is too heavy — that He will give us rest.

Jesus had promised me in this verse that if I would bend my neck under His yoke and let Him be my teacher, I would find Him a gentle taskmaster. With His yoke on my shoulders, I had been promised I would find rest unto my soul.

I obediently went on vacation. One of the older ladies of the church, who was virtually a grandma to our family, took care of our 14-year-old son, Mark, and our 11-year-old daughter, Patrece, so they could stay in school. My wife and I headed out to the Oregon coast with our minds filled with concern about the future.

I sought God.

I prayed.

I played.

I relaxed.

I made up my mind to get well.

But after several days, it was plain to us that the doctor's prescribed "vacation therapy" was not having any dramatic effect. My speech was becoming more slurred every day.

We decided Violet needed to get back to the kids. On our way home, we stopped at a store to pick up a few souvenirs for Mark and Patrece. As I went up to the counter to pay for the items, I began having trouble communicating with the clerk. I was giving her money, and she kept pushing it back. She looked a little scared and stepped back from the counter. Apparently she didn't want to take any money until I got out the full amount.

I'm not sure what the problem was, but I am sure the more I tried to hurry under her alarmed stare, the more inarticulate I became.

As we got back into the car and drove off, Violet and I started to laugh about it. We thought how funny it was that she didn't seem to want to take my money — but it was a nervous laughter.

Then all of a sudden my laughter turned into tears. I began to weep so hard that I had to pull the car off to the side of the road.

Violet said, "What's wrong?"

I said, "I don't know."

We both cried. We just sobbed and sobbed.

Once we reached home, I began thinking that I would like to go fishing in the mountains of Oregon and try to get some additional rest. We decided one of the kids should go with me. Since Mark was at a more crucial age for school work, we decided Patrece should accompany me.

We fished and hiked and paddled around in a rowboat.

I did not know that it was becoming obvious to my little girl that I was getting progressively worse. Every day, she became more worried.

Here is how Patrece remembers it:

> About six weeks before Dad became very ill, Mom and Dad went on a trip. I didn't know that anything was wrong, I just thought Dad was tired.
>
> Then he and I went fishing at Camp Davidson up in the mountains. I remember when we started out on the trip how I was so excited and didn't have a care in the world.
>
> Then the longer Dad and I were together, I knew deep down inside something was really wrong.
>
> I remember being out in the rowboat fishing with Dad and he was having a really hard time talking. We needed to go back to shore because it had started raining. Dad was crying, and I felt so hopeless. I thought that making him row the boat was too much on him, but I was too little to do it myself.
>
> Inside I felt like I was an adult and

needed to take care of my dad, but outside I couldn't do anything.

During that same trip, we were driving one day and decided to take this road that had our last name. We turned down the road and got stuck in the snow. It took forever to dig our way out, and I kept thinking that all the stress was going to kill my dad.

Here I was, supposed to be taking care of him, and instead he kept having to work so hard. I didn't know how to do anything differently. I couldn't figure out how I was supposed to go about taking care of my dad, but I couldn't drop the feeling that I was supposed to do it.

One frozen morning, I had gone out for a walk, and when I returned to our cabin, little Patrece was bundled up under a puffy quilt bathed in sunshine. She gave me the most incredible smile, and I realized what a treasure this beautiful child was — what a wonderful gift from God.

She loved her daddy so. And I loved her. This was a smile I would tuck away in my heart — a beautiful smile to treasure for the rest of my life.

One day, I called home and tried to talk to Violet, but she could not understand anything I was trying to say.

Violet became very scared. "When Duane called me," she remembers, "his speech was so inarticulate that I could not understand one word he said."

I had said, "Get home now."

There was nothing wrong with my mental capacities, and I could still drive just fine. I continued to attend church with my family.

One afternoon over the Memorial Day weekend, a

few days after Patrece and I got home from the mountains, I was standing in front of our fireplace. I was rubbing my right ear — I do that a lot when I am thinking — and it dawned on me that I was numb on my right side.

I couldn't feel anything.

My sister, Joy Ann, who was visiting that day, saw everything and alerted Violet. They got me to the car and rushed me to the hospital.

In the crowded, bustling emergency room, the nurses did not make us wait like they do most of the time in trauma centers. They immediately got me onto a table in an examining cubicle and summoned doctors who began trying to figure out what was happening.

By now, I was paralyzed on my right side. My mouth was drooping, and I could barely talk.

One doctor took a pencil and ran it along the bottom of my foot to see how I would react.

I didn't.

He said, "There are obviously some neurological problems here. Let's hospitalize you and run several more tests."

One of the tests, the CAT scan, showed a dark blob, which to the doctors looked like a possible tumor. However, something was strange about it. The radiologist giving the CAT scan kept looking at it and then said, within Violet's hearing, "I've seen too many of these pictures to think it's a tumor. Something is different."

Next, they scheduled an angiogram, which consists of shooting dye into the arteries, veins, and capillaries. They then take an x-ray and determine the exact location of the problem. They told Violet I would be back in my room in about 30 minutes.

But it would take much longer.

Something about the angiogram itself seemed to affect me very negatively. The doctors grew puzzled.

When, after three hours, I had not come back, Violet knew that something was terribly wrong.

Indeed, I had regained the use of my right side, but during the angiogram, the paralysis returned.

By the time I was wheeled back into my room, I was extremely confused and irritated.

The doctors began asking me questions to try and figure out what had happened to me during the angiogram. However, my speech was worse than ever, and all I could do was scowl.

Violet remembers asking me if I was angry. At that time the question dumbfounded me; I did not realize how I was acting.

My paralysis slowly left, and a little bit of speech returned. But what had happened, at least for the moment, remained a mystery.

They kept talking about a tumor.

We called Mark into the room. Violet told him that I was going to have to have an operation.

"The Sunday my dad became paralyzed," remembers Patrece. "I was at a friend's house. My mom called and explained how serious it was and made arrangements for me to stay with my girlfriend. Mom didn't really tell me much."

Patrece was a seventh-grader in her first year of junior high school, and she understood much more than we thought she did.

Mark, on the other hand, was 14, a high school freshman who, in many ways, was already a man. As he listened to Violet's words, he stared at me with serious eyes — his thoughts deep and grim.

His biology class had just studied the human brain, and he knew that bad things can happen when doctors cut through the human skull. He knew the violent reaction that could take place if the brain is touched by any foreign object.

Mark told me, "Dad, this is serious."

I felt like saying, "You don't think I know that, son?" But I didn't say it.

I'll never forget what he did next. Here was a kid who was almost as tall as me, a boy who had been raised in church, and he said to me, "Dad, we ought to pray."

I was lying in the bed, and I don't think I said anything. My boy crawled up on that bed, just like the prophet laying himself on the son. He just stretched his hands out over my hands, and then he put his feet onto mine. And he began to pray. I can't remember what his prayer was because I was so filled with emotion and confusion and trauma over what was happening.

But he had the assurance, and after he prayed for me, he held me. He did not move. He just held his father.

Then, being the 14 year old that he was, he sprang off of that bed, stood back, smiled and gave me the two-thumbs-up sign, and said, "It's going to be okay, Dad."

P O S T C A R D

F I V E

Something Different

"We're going to go in for a tumor — what appears to be a manasioma tumor," the doctors said.

Two doctors were going to do the surgery. They began to discuss with Violet and me the procedure to make sure we understood everything. They drew a picture for us to show exactly where they would go in, how much of the skull they would have to cut out, and what they were going to do once inside the cranium.

Feeling the tumor was laying right on top of the brain, they told us they would try to lift it off without touching the brain any more than necessary — so as not to cause swelling.

I remember that I felt completely rational about undergoing an operation to fix what was wrong with me. I thought, *Fine, brain surgery. Let's get it done, and then we can get on with life.*

I think Violet was feeling the same way because one of the doctors took her into another room and told her very seriously, "We have the feeling you are not grasping this. Your husband is not going to come out any different than he goes in. We want you to know that. We have the feeling you think he's going to be all right as soon as the surgery is over. We want you to know there's a possibility that he might never be able to talk again."

They were trying to prepare Violet for the worst, but the way she was looking at it, nothing could be worse than the months we had just gone through — not knowing what was wrong as I got worse and worse. Living with such uncertainty had been almost unbearable.

Now that the doctors knew what action they wanted to take, it was almost a relief. Okay, let's get it fixed, let's go on! But I really had no idea what lay ahead. Neither did Violet.

The doctors left the room, and Violet hugged me. I didn't say a word. I couldn't. Suddenly, we were both crying. We just wept out of fear of the unknown. What was going to happen?

A lay member of my church visited me before my surgery. I could tell that he was wanting to say something but was having difficulty.

If nothing else, it was good to see somebody else having difficulty expressing themselves.

He was clearing his throat and talking about the weather and trying to make light conversation.

But here I was, barely able to speak, facing a major

surgery, and I wasn't concerned about the weather, or whether the lake was up or down, or whether the salmon were running — I wanted some answers from God. I had sought God, and I had prepared my heart.

So, he said to me, "What sin have you committed that you are in this bed?"

As best as I could, I let him know that I didn't know of any such sin. But, if he had the Holy Spirit's supernatural gift of knowledge, then I wanted to hear what God was saying to me.

I was certainly in no position to refuse to repent.

"Tell me if you know," I struggled out. I wasn't trying to be a smart aleck. I was reaching out.

Well, he left convinced I must have done something terrible that I was unwilling to confess to a concerned Christian brother.

But I really could not imagine any sin so enormous that God would strike me down like this. I was confused.

Violet was unsure of what tomorrow would bring — when I would go under the knife. We were both scared.

Our faith was still strong, but that didn't make the situation any less terrifying. We were being jerked around by the absolute unknown — and everything kept changing at a terrifying pace.

One minute, I had been an ambitious, successful pastor of a growing church. The next, I was weeping a lot — not being able to pronounce my words — and even drooled occasionally. Why? Because I was mentally exhausted, according to the first doctor. So, I had tried to get some rest.

The hours and days that followed my second diagnosis are a swirl of images and impressions in my clouded memory. There are things that I remember in a half-dream, half-reality. For example, in the early morning before my surgery, I sensed that death had come into my room.

I became quite concerned. It was there. It was real. Death, waiting for me.

Well, I did not want to go.

So, I began to pray — fervently. Now, I cannot tell you if this all took place over several hours or in a matter of minutes. However, as I remember it, I got out of my bed and went over to a chair in the middle of the room and knelt there, using it as an altar, with my elbows on that chair.

I remember praying these words: "Come, God, let us reason together. This isn't wise what You are going to allow to happen to me."

Well, that was mighty bold, wouldn't you say? I was informing the Almighty Ruler of the universe and Creator of all things as to what was wise and what was not.

You see, I was proud of my way with words. That was one reason that my new inability to speak coherently was so galling. Among my peers, I had been dubbed "The Golden Tongue Orator."

You may find this hard to believe, but at night in my dreams, I used to ponder new words that I had heard during the day before. I would wake up with the new words, and the first thing I would do would be to go to the dictionary and look them up.

Then, of course, I would use them. So, I was quite the wordsmith, inserting terms such as "emotive" and "conundrum" and "exegesis" into idle conversation. I enjoyed impressing my peers by using difficult words that I had heard.

"Well," I would say as offhandedly as possible,

"would you say that the non-loquacious groans of Romans 8:26 are always of a glossolalic nature?"

So here I was kneeling beside this hospital chair, acting as my lawyer, presenting my case to the High Judge. I knew that God was listening to me pray, because you cannot pray without God listening. He is always a listener to our prayers.

But He wasn't responding — not as far as I could tell.

So I expanded my argument. I said, "I'm a husband. What's Violet going to do without me?"

No response.

"I have two kids. They're not going to want to live without a father."

Total silence from heaven.

So I said, "Okay, God, this is my last reason." I had saved my big cannon for the last. I said, "God, You know that You called me to this church, and this church is growing, and we are giving more money than ever before to Your work. And look at all that we are doing for foreign missions. What are these people going to do without me?"

Then I heard my first response.

I heard laughter from heaven.

God spoke to my heart and in His still, small voice told me, "Son, I don't need you. But you sure do need Me."

I will never forget that answer as long as I live.

I got up from that altar in my room on the sixth floor of the hospital. For some reason, I noticed for the first time that my room number was 668.

Six stands for the number of man, I remember thinking, eight stands for the number of new beginnings.

God seemed to speak to my heart, "Duane, I have a new beginning for you."

I walked over to the window and in the moonlight gazed down at the hospital lawn's giant fir trees.

As I looked at those beautiful trees, I formed a cup in my hands, and I said, "God, these represent Your hands. I put my life in Your hands. You can take care of Violet. You can take care of Mark and Patrece. You can take care of the church. If You want to take me home, I'm ready to go home. However, if You want me to remain on earth and continue the work that You put me on earth to do, I promise You that I will say, be, and do what You want me to do all the days of my life."

And I felt peace for the first time.

I looked around and no longer sensed death in my room. What had been there before? An evil spirit? The death angel? I don't know.

But I know that my prayer was real and fervent — as was God's calm answer.

That night, Violet also lay awake in bed.

"Lord, what if it's Your time to take him?" she asked. "What would I do?"

She was scared to live without me. Scared even to face the possibility. She told God she couldn't go on living if I died.

Unable to sleep, she got up and did some laundry. Here is how she described that awful night to me:

> I picked up one of your shirts. Honey, you know you have a certain smell that gets mixed in with the after-shave you use? Well, I smelled one of your shirts, and the thought came to me, *What if Duane does die? What would I do? I wouldn't have this.* I smelled your shirt again and held it close to my cheek — and began

to cry. The idea that you might not come home had finally sunk in.

I went back to bed, but I lay there awake. I kept milling over everything in my mind, things such as, would I stay in Oregon or would I go live near my parents? Would I try to keep the house? What would I do about the car? Should I go back to school — or should I conserve our little savings for the kids' college and immediately get a job to support us?

What would I do? I asked myself. But I had no answers. So I finally said, "God . . ."

I don't even know how to say what happened, but I just turned it all over to Him. I said, "It's just entirely up to You." And at that moment, I knew you were going to live, Duane. The minute I did that, I felt the assurance that you were going to live.

That simple conversation with the Lord helped me walk through everything. It wasn't me, it was God holding me up through the entire ordeal. It was that assurance that I got that night, that peace that washed over me. I did not hear an audible voice, but I just knew you were going to live.

At the same time that I was surrendering to God, Violet was giving me up to Him as well. We both prayed almost the same prayer.

I call it our prayer of relinquishment. I relinquished my life, my authority, my rulership, my everything to God. She relinquished me as her husband and the father of her children.

The Spirit, although He is not seen, was present to produce the same effect in both of our lives — an incredible peace. I knew that I was going to live. Violet knew that I was going to live. But we had no idea the supernatural strength it would take to survive the next 10 years.

Yet, we faced the next day calmly because we had the assurance, that peace of God that surpasses all understanding.

I fell asleep until the orderly came in and woke me. He said, "I'm here to give you your haircut."

I wisecracked — although the words came out with enormous difficulty, "Hey, this isn't a barber shop." I am not sure that he understood.

In fact, by that time, I was uttering a lot of garble — saying such nonsense as "Peas kill me" when in fact I was trying to say, "Please have my dad call me when I get out of surgery."

So, I held up the menu from which patients ordered breakfast, lunch, and dinner everyday. I struggled out, "No haircut on this."

The orderly grinned at me, getting my silly joke — the menu did not include haircuts.

"Hey," he said, "you don't want to take away my fun, do you?"

The orderly clipped off all of my hair. Then he got his razor and shaved my scalp. He stood and admired his work — as if he were Michelangelo or Picasso or somebody. Then he asked me, "Do you want to take a look?"

I shook my head. I certainly did not.

But my curiosity got the best of me so I peeked in the mirror. It was awful.

To release the tension, Violet brought me a lollipop and told me that I looked like a spiritual Kojak.

My next memory is of lying on the gurney — the rolling stretcher on which patients are pushed from place to place. I was already groggy from my medication, but I was filled with enormous peace.

I felt the prayers of hundreds of people who cared about me and knew that at that moment, I was about to go under the knife. Since I had been in the ministry for almost 25 years, I was known a lot of places. Friends of the ministry were lifting me up in prayer all over the country and around the world. Many had come into my hospital room days before the surgery and laid hands on me and interceded to God on my behalf.

I could feel their intercession now.

And I was very, very relaxed.

In the distant fog of my memories of that day, I clearly remember trying to talk and joke with the doctors — although in reality I'm not sure I was all that capable of joking with anybody. However, I recall being pushed through the hallways of the hospital completely at peace.

A Christian doctor, Ben Wilson, who was doing his internship at St. Vincent Hospital in Portland, asked the neurosurgeon heading up the surgical team if he could observe my operation. He was there the whole time and went out and reported to Violet every few hours what was happening. So my wife knew, even before the procedure was over, that they were not finding what they expected.

He was a blessing and comfort to Violet. "The operation took about eight hours," remembers Violet.

She also remembers the shock of stepping up to my bedside in the intensive care unit and seeing my head — swollen beyond recognition. Fluid had built up between my skull and my scalp, giving it a ghastly, misshapen look.

She thought, as she looked at the left side of my face, so swollen that it seemed to rest upon my left shoulder — "Is this my husband?"

She glanced down at the chart at the foot of the bed. "Parrish," it read.

"This is my husband," she mused. "But will he ever be the same?"

"I had a real need to be with Duane," she remembers. "He looked so vulnerable: His head was shaved, tubes protruded everywhere, and only a piece of gauze with yellow disinfectant covered his stitches."

I was unconscious, but I kept reaching up with my hand and pushing on the back of my neck. Violet would take my hand away, afraid I would do some damage. I kept pushing, so Violet asked the nurse if she could give me something for my obvious pain.

The nurse said, "No, we can't give him anything because then his vital signs wouldn't show up right."

The doctors had anticipated a benign tumor.

I am told that the standard procedure with a tumor is to go in and try to lift it off without touching the brain any more than necessary — so as not to cause swelling.

Although they kept looking, the doctors found no tumor. They did find what was described to us as an "arteriovenous malformation." Here was a new word for the "wordsmith." I was hoping I would never have to learn the meaning.

The medical encyclopedia defines an arteriovenous malformation, also called an "AV malformation" for short, as a blood vessel in the brain that can rupture and cause death or brain damage similar to a stroke. It is a dangerous condition suffered by only 2,500 patients a year in the United States — quite a small number in comparison to other causes of illness.

In my case, one tiny capillary — a very small blood vessel — had not actually ruptured but, instead, had leaked off and on for several years, which explained the many adhesions around one small capillary. The doctors told Violet that the last time it had ruptured, the capillary must have continued to leak for about a year to form a clot the size of a man's fist.

They told us they had never seen anything like it. Usually, an AV malformation will spring a big enough leak to pour sufficient blood into the brain to cause paralysis, tipping off doctors to go in and take care of it quickly. In such cases, the healing process is much faster than in my situation.

My AV malformation's growing clot had smothered or "corroded" a small part of my brain, causing "necrosis" or tissue death. The doctors had to suction away some dead brain matter. The brain is about the consistency of mashed potatoes, making it extremely fragile.

Now they knew the reason their angiogram had caused me temporary paralysis and such excruciating pain in my teeth. The dye they had pumped in for the test had put the capillary's leak under pressure, making it leak more, pressing on the clot. This caused even more pressure on the brain.

After the surgeons had found the AV malformation and suctioned away the dead tissue, they had cut down into my brain three or four times.

Why?

Were they looking for a tumor?

We were never told!

But as a result, my brain suffered quite a bit of

trauma. Just as my son had learned in school, my brain reacted violently and swelled much more than it would have ordinarily.

And much more brain damage resulted.

Were my doctors incompetent? Was I a victim of malpractice? No. I prefer to give them the benefit of the doubt. My best interests were their prime concern. Since it was such a unique AV malformation, they were looking for anything else out of the ordinary.

Many people who experience such extensive trauma as I did never recover their speech.

They never speak again.

But God had something else in mind for me.

Fighting Back

I was in severe pain the first day after I came out of surgery.

Violet became absolutely exhausted and decided that there was little she could do for me, so she left me in God's hands and went home.

"When I left you that night," my wife tells me now, "you didn't look good. But then, I'm a novice. I haven't been in hospitals that much."

She had no choice but to trust the professionals.

So, she went home and got a night's sleep. When she returned at the crack of dawn, she says, "I headed straight for the intensive care unit, but I was told that you had been taken to a private room."

Immediately something in her spirit said, "This is not right." She thought, *That is strange.*

"When I went up and saw you in your room," she remembers, "Duane, you looked much worse than you had when you first came out of surgery."

Indeed, the swelling and pain had worsened. I was urgently reaching up with my hand and pushing on my neck, just as I had before.

"That upset me," remembers my wife, "I went to talk to the nurse and asked if she could give you something. She said, 'Well, your husband just now got in his room. His paperwork is still getting here, but I think so.'"

The nurse waited until my chart got there and gave me something to ease the pain.

Violet's sister, who had rushed in from out of town, was staying with our children. She came up to the hospital and thought it might be a good idea for Violet to have a break.

She had forgotten to bring a dress for church on Sunday, so she said, "It would be good for you to get out, why don't you come with me and help me find a dress?"

The nurse said, "You might as well go. What I've given him was quite strong. He will be out for several hours. He won't even know you're gone."

So the two of them went to the mall. There they ran into a preacher friend and his wife who said they were on their way up to see me.

"I know this was God," remembers Violet. "It was no coincidence that we bumped into them. They saw how concerned I was, so they assured me they would go sit with Duane until I could get back to the hospital."

When the pastor and his wife arrived, I was in trouble.

Fluid had built up between my scalp and skull. My brain was swelling inside my cranium, pushing on the piece of skull that had been sawed-off and wired back on with something resembling fishing leader.

I was in distress.

The surgeons needed to rush me back into surgery. It was very serious. In fact, it was life threatening. I was on the verge of death.

But before the doctors could go back in and relieve the pressure, hospital legal procedure required that they obtain Violet's permission.

"They needed my signature, but I wasn't there," remembers my wife regretfully. "Duane's dad was the only other one who could sign. He had gone to the hospital chapel to pray, not suspecting that the staff was searching frantically for one of us to sign."

This pastor friend and his wife came in while all this was going on and told the nurse that Violet was probably still at the mall.

"When I heard the page over the mall intercom, I panicked" says my wife. "I just knew Duane had died. They didn't explain anything on the page or give any message to anyone at the mall except 'Get to the hospital right away.' "

When Violet arrived at the hospital, she found that my dad had been located and had already given them his signature. I was already in emergency surgery.

There, they put a shunt in to help drain off some of the fluid and gave me medicine to try to bring down the swelling. They also put in a monitoring device touching my brain, so they could monitor the swelling accurately.

After the emergency surgery, they put me back into the intensive care unit and watched me closely all night. The shunt and medicine seemed to be working. The swelling went down, and I was out of immediate danger.

However, I stayed in intensive care in a coma for five days.

It was a tough, long five days for Violet. One of the worst things was how the kids kept begging to see me. I think they wanted to be reassured that I was still alive.

When Patrece was allowed to come in to see me, she just came unglued. Here is how she remembers it:

> I missed my mom and dad, and I really didn't know what was going on.
>
> Finally, when I was taken to the hospital, my dad had already undergone surgery. My mom was trying to prepare me for what was going on, and what my dad was going to look like, but I thought that she was being silly. I knew that no matter what had happened, he would still be my dad.
>
> But when I walked down to the room and looked in, I started to scream. That was not my dad. He was all bruised and distorted. He had tubes all over him. He was not my dad. The last time I had seen my dad he had thick brown hair, a huge smile, and lots of life and laughter. I don't think anyone could have prepared me for the way he looked that day.

Patrece hadn't expected to see me hooked up to every machine you can think of — and tubes in my nose and throat.

After five long days, I awoke just as if I had been sleeping for a few hours.

When the tube was taken out of my throat, I tried to speak and realized I couldn't articulate. Not even as much (or little, I should say) as before the surgery.

When the doctors explained that my speech loss might be permanent, I plunged into depths of a sadness I can't begin to explain. The old me had died, and I hated this poor substitute.

I remember that I looked around and saw the nurse, the doctor, my associate pastor, and my wife. I wanted to express what was on my mind. But I could not.

I could not utter a word.

I wanted to know things like, How long have I been asleep? What's going on at the church? I wanted to get a report from my associate. I wanted to see Mark and let him see that I was okay. I wanted to kiss Patrece and stroke her hair.

But, my vocabulary had been reduced to two words: "O God."

It was no profanity. I was not cursing Him.

It was a prayer.

It was a plea.

O God.

What had happened to me?

O God

Slowly my strength came back. At first I just sat up in bed, then in a chair, then I started walking. This happened in the first week or two.

However, my vocabulary continued to be only "O God."

When I wanted to express my thoughts, the only words that would come out were, "O God."

It didn't dawn on me at first, but later on I became so appreciative for those two words. Of all the words in the English language, God left me with the two most wonderful words in any language: O God.

I became known as the patient who walked around the hospital halls whistling the hymns of the church. I whistled "Great is Thy Faithfulness," one of my favorite hymns. Then when I would come to the end of the hymn, and I would say, "O God, O God, O God."

One day, a therapist and the doctors came into the room and tested me on math. They asked me, "What is two plus two?"

I wanted to get this right. I tried so hard. I wanted to prove to them that I could still function and that my God was a great God who was healing me miraculously.

"What is two plus two?" they repeated.

I was determined to show them that I could bounce back faster than they ever dreamed, with God's help.

"What is two plus two?"

I thought and thought and I thought. Then I got a smile on my face, and I lifted up five fingers. The look on their faces let me know that I had failed the test.

They put a pen in my hand and asked me to write my name. But, I couldn't even do that.

There was no need for the doctors to say more. I knew I was in trouble.

My brain was just not the same.

But I was still inside there — fighting to come out and show everybody that I was still me.

I still had my sense of humor. I began to think, *Well, now I can't talk — just think how many people that's going to make happy.* I chuckled to myself.

So what if I can't write, I told myself. *Well,* I snickered to myself, *I'll never have to worry about writing letters again.*

Then I said to myself, *Well, at least I can read the Bible and get some consolation from the Word of God. That will help. That will make me feel better.*

So I reached for my Bible, which Violet had put on the night stand. I opened it up at random, and when my eyes fell on the text, I realized the terrible truth.

I couldn't read.

I guess that was when it finally started to hit me. I was terribly disabled. I was a handicapped preacher, unable to speak and doomed to never preach again or help sinners find Jesus.

The written page no longer made any sense to me — which was absolutely baffling.

It was as if I had been taken to my own personal Tower of Babel. In my case, I still understood completely what people were saying, but I could not respond. Written words were completely foreign to me. Handwriting on my chart or in books might as well have been Chinese or Swahili or chicken scratching.

My paralysis was gone, but when I gripped a pencil, my ability to sign my name, to jot down the simplest thought, or write a single word was gone.

I was trapped — imprisoned. Just imagine what it would be like if you suddenly could not say a word, write anything, read anything, or communicate beyond improvised sign language and desperate facial expressions.

It was terrifying.

My mind was still active, but I could not quiz my doctors. I could not tell my wife that I loved her.

I could not read my mail nor write checks. I could not explain our finances to Violet, nor ask whether she had changed the oil in the car, nor ask if she had followed up on this or that thing in progress when I went into surgery.

A terrible depression rushed over me.

Its weight crushed me.

I remember thinking, *God, I don't understand. All I was wanting was more of You. What's going on?*

Sensing how depressed I was, LeeRoy Hunt, former pastor of Christian Life Center, in Aloha, Oregon, (a neighboring city to Beaverton) began coming up to see me every morning before he went to his office. For the rest of my hospital stay, he would come up and read the Word of God for me. It was powerful.

I will treasure forever the sight of him walking back and forth in my room while he read aloud from the Bible. It was a gift of more value than he could imagine.

Another visitor that meant so much to me was Ron Mell, author of the book, *Surprise Endings*, and pastor of the Four Square Church in Beaverton. When he would leave my hospital room, my spirit said, "You can make it."

The doctors realized I could still think things through, that I was completely aware of everything around me, and that I was still reasoning effectively.

They felt the part of my brain that gave strength to my tongue, to my soft palate, and to my cheeks, was destroyed so that I could not hold them firm enough to form words. My swallowing was also affected, so much so I could not drink liquid without choking.

My associate pastor, Greg Hickman, had to take over most of my duties at the church. One day before I was released from the hospital he came to see me, and he was very nervous. I thought it was kind of funny.

I realized he was informing me that the church board had taken away my authority to sign checks.

Well, that was no terrible thing! I couldn't write anything, much less produce a signature that the bank would accept.

The church's checking account required two sig-natures on our checks, but I couldn't write and they had to pay the bills. So they had put his name on the signature authorization card at the bank.

Greg felt so bad about it that he apologized over

and over. "I'm not trying to take over the church," he assured me. "Please, this was the board's decision."

I tried to tell him that I completely understood. "Don't worry," I wanted to say — but could not. "Don't worry about it. Things at the church can't be put on hold forever!"

I think he saw the approval in my eyes.

Because his youth group was very large for a church our size, I knew Greg and his wife, Roxanne, had been well prepared for the responsibilities they now had to assume. He did a fantastic job filling all the duties of a pastor in the office and behind my pulpit.

How I longed to return there.

But, it was okay with me if Greg filled my shoes for a while.

POSTCARD EIGHT

Denial

For a year I had ignored the symptoms that finally resulted in the brain surgery that totally changed my life. As I lay in bed, I began to reflect on the physical symptoms I had denied.

If I was holding a coffee cup, sometimes my hand would start to turn. If I was talking to somebody, and I was not paying attention to my cup, it would just slowly start to turn, sometimes spilling on me. Hold that hand straight, I would chide myself when I noticed my hand starting to turn. Consciously, I would make it turn back. When I would start to swallow liquid, I would cough and choke unexpectedly.

One night, I remember distinctly, I fixed myself a bowl of peaches. I walked into the living room and sat down in the chair. Then, my hand slowly turned without my realizing it so that I spilled the whole bowl of peaches in my lap. I got so mad at myself.

I was bumping into doors, too. As I went through a door casing, I would bump into it. There was nothing wrong with my vision. It was more a loss of coordination. I would say to myself, *Well, stupid, what did you do that for?*

My work was piling up at church. I was not completing tasks that needed my attention the most, and I was easily distracted.

As Violet and I talked, we both decided that I had been feeling the pressure of a minor business deal gone bad.

So I thought, *Well, that's what's wrong with me. That's why I'm so under the gun.*

Meanwhile, though, I was majoring in minors. Minor things would become so important to me. I picked at them as if they really mattered the most. Yet if my wife brought me major challenges that I needed to see right away, I would not want to face them.

Christmas of 1979, family members who hadn't seen me in quite a while noticed changes, also. They came up to Violet, saying, "What's wrong with Duane?"

She would ask, "What do you mean?"

They would answer, "Well, he's so touchy and temperamental with the kids."

That was unusual because I was always the one to get down on the floor with all my nieces and nephews and play with them. Now all of a sudden, I was telling them, "Out of my way," and "Go behave," and "Do this and do that."

The changes in me had been so gradual that Violet and I hardly noticed. Friends and loved ones, however, could tell something was wrong.

As more and more people privately advised me that I was behaving strangely, deep down in my spirit I was troubled.

I began to reflect back to the beginning of 1979, or around that time. I had been at Christ Center for about six years. I was sitting at my desk having my daily devotions with the Lord, and I thought to myself, I'm sick and tired of playing church.

During my childhood, I had seen God move through godly leaders. Now, I longed for a spontaneous move of the Holy Spirit that would convict, captivate, reveal sins, and deliver Christians into the joy of the Lord.

I longed for the Holy Spirit to flow, anointing us with gladness. As I sat there in my study, I realized deep in my soul that I wanted to see a real move of the Spirit of God — not something manufactured.

I saw that I had gotten into a routine; I suppose just going through the motions. I realized I wanted to feel more, learn more, and experience more.

I turned to one of the Psalms where David wrote, "I want to know your ways, your truths, and walk in your paths."

"Yes," I whispered, "God, I want to do that. I want to walk in Your paths. I want to know Your ways, not my own." I felt such emptiness.

There had been times when I had, indeed, sensed the presence of God in our services. I had seen people held spellbound by the moving of the Holy Ghost. It hadn't resulted from a polished performance or happened because of professionalism. It was the Holy Spirit that moved in a sovereign way, convicting and changing people's lives.

Oh, how I longed for that to be the norm!

I had been reading A.W. Tozer's book, *The Pursuit of God*, and that day I reached for it and turned to a chapter that closed with a written prayer that had touched me. It went something like this: "I have tasted of your goodness. It has both satisfied and made me thirsty for more. Oh, God, I long to be filled with longings." In my mind I understood that word "longings."

I closed that book and I began to stare at the wall in deep thought.

Longings.

What were my longings?

I thought about all my desires. I wanted Christ Center to be the biggest church in Oregon and give the most money of any of our churches to missions.

Then, I said, "I want to shoot a 72 in golf." For all you non-golfers, the lower the score, the better.

I longed to bag a seven-point bull elk on a hunting trip and have it mounted on my office wall so other preachers would come in and exclaim what a great hunter I was.

Realizing my motivations were all stemming from self and to make me look good, I was grieved in my spirit that I did not have substantial longings for God.

So, I said, "God, I want to have a longing for a closer relationship with You."

I was not worried about my salvation. I knew that I was saved. I knew that I was in good shape spiritually if the Lord were to call me to heaven.

But I was filled with guilt that I called myself a man of God, a spiritual leader, a pastor of people, yet I did not hunger and thirst for more of the Lord I served. I mourned that there was no substantial yearning in my heart to experience more of God. So, I said, "God, I want more of You."

Now, I am almost ashamed to confess that I expected God to come down right then and there — that very morning — and give me my desire. I expected at least a glowing tingle. I thought I might see an angel or have God touch me on the shoulder and say, "My son, let me share this or that eternal truth with you."

But it didn't happen that way.

Instead, God allowed something else.

I found myself in a hospital bed, unable to speak, unable to minister, unable to be the pastor I once was.

Disabled.

But not defeated.

The "Speak and Spell" Drilling

As I convalesced in the hospital, I still had lots of questions — nagging questions to which I had already been given answers, but which returned to trouble me anyway. My emotions soared and crashed.

One thing that helped me so much was the continued faithfulness of my friends — pastor friends and lay members of Christ Center — who dropped by my room to pray for me. Two couples in particular, friends of ours in the ministry, really interceded for me — Gordon and Teri Myers, and Dale and Sherri Edwards. I will always be grateful for them.

I am ashamed to say that even as people were

holding me up to God, I cried out to Him, impatient that I was not yet healed, yet at the same time thankful for my constant progress.

Then one day the doctor gave me what should have been "good news" that I was going home.

Two months had passed since my second surgery. I had undergone speech therapy every single day, but I found it hard to accept that I was going home before I was completely restored.

I wasn't the only one who had difficulty with the news.

"I can remember liking to go up to the hospital but not staying in the room where my dad was," says Patrece. "I wasn't used to feeling sorry for him, and I didn't want to accept this new dad I had. I was trying to live my life denying everything that was happening, but I couldn't do that anymore now that Dad was being released to come home."

"Dad had become foreign to me," remembers Mark. "I didn't understand him. I wanted to help and do my part, but I didn't know what to do."

Patrece described the night before I was to come home from the hospital:

> I remember Mom sitting me and my brother down and telling us that we would go pick Dad up tomorrow. I was screaming inside, *No, No! This is not my dad that we are bringing back. The man in the hospital isn't my dad.*
>
> I never let Mom and Dad see what I was feeling. I didn't want to load them down with more stuff, but that night I cried all night long. I was scared, hurt, confused — I loved my dad

and could never hurt him, but I also couldn't accept him because I hurt too bad every time I saw him like that.

The fact that the doctors were sending me home raised a fear I'd been trying so hard to ignore. Maybe I would never be completely healed.

Sensing how I was feeling, my sister tried to think of ways to advance my skills. She bought me the children's game, Speak and Spell.

When I pushed a button, the toy said, "DOG!" It was then up to me to try and spell D-O-G. The thing was merciless. If I typed in G-U-G, it would announce to the entire world that I was WRONG, and that I should have typed D-O-G. As ridiculous as it may seem, that Speak and Spell was exactly what I needed.

My kids would sit with me and drill me. B-U-T? WRONG! D-U-T? WRONG! D-U-G? WRONG!

D-O-G?

RIGHT!

"We would sit for hours at a time playing Speak and Spell with him," remembers Patrece.

I had a terrible fear that Violet would give up on me.

"I'm still here," she would assure me. "I have no plans to go anywhere."

It was not always easy for her.

When I got back home, I wanted to be around people. I had always been a people person, and I wanted to continue. The doctors encouraged this because it would force me to try to communicate. The more people around you, the more you have to try to talk.

But there was a down side to that.

I would work so hard to try to make conversation that it wore me down. After they left, I was exhausted and just needed to be alone in my thoughts. I wouldn't even try to talk with my kids or my wife because I was drained physically, mentally, and emotionally. I was just so tired of trying to talk. Every word was an effort to get out.

Sometimes I would sit for hours in the living room by myself. Violet would be in the kitchen fixing dinner and slowly it would grow dark, and I wouldn't even lean over and turn on the lamp. I would just sit in the total darkness.

Mark came home a number of times after school and would bound into the room — only to be startled that I was sitting there silently in the dark. He didn't even know what to say to me — sitting there, not even looking up at him.

He would mumble a half-hearted greeting and go to his room.

I grew tired very easily, which brought on what must have seemed like moodiness and what was a very demanding attitude toward Violet. I took her for granted and certainly did not realize that she was experiencing a hellish lifestyle that spouses of Alzheimer's Disease victims refer to as "the 48-hour day." Her every waking minute was filled with me, my demands, my complaints, my problems, and my needs.

She had to be nearby at all times. I would panic if I sensed she was not in earshot. It got really bad when she could not even close the door to the bathroom without hearing me outside, nervous, knocking, asking if she was there. I felt much better if she left the door open.

She had absolutely no time for herself.

I was like a demanding toddler. I did not care about

her needs at all. I wanted her to be available for me.

"I would realize that I needed to be more patient, and I would pray for patience," Violet remembers.

"He was just so extremely slow —" slow-moving, slow in reacting, and slow in recovering, she said later. "I was still my same old self. I would whip around the house and clean up and cook, but he would want me to stop and be with him. Things were fine until I became exhausted, then I would snap at him, and the guilt would follow."

It was not easy for any of us to maintain a positive attitude — or to walk in faith believing that everything would eventually return to normal.

"I became distant from the Lord and my family," Mark says. "I can't really remember a lot of what happened. There was a lot of pain and feelings that I had that led me astray. There were emotions that I needed to deal with and never did — I avoided and ignored them."

For 12-year-old Patrece, my recovery was not all inspiration and joy either. She recalls:

> I was very frustrated at times because Dad would always insist on doing things himself. If we were out trying to order a hamburger at McDonald's for instance, he would insist on doing it himself no matter how long it took and no matter how many people would stare.
>
> He would not allow me or Mom or anybody to help. That got to be embarrassing at times, but we never let him know we were embarrassed. These were just feelings that went on inside of us.
>
> He would also get very frustrated at me because I would try and jump in and finish his

sentences for him. Of course, we didn't realize at the time the best thing Dad could be doing was doing everything himself.

During my recovery, everybody was always making over me. Of course, I ate it up. Furthermore, I got to be the hero, earning high praises from the doctors and our friends. I was the one whom people felt sorry for, yet it was Violet who got stuck behind the scenes, unappreciated, unthanked — taking care of me, coming along behind me to pick up, and trying to be both mother and father to our kids.

Here's how Violet remembers those trying times:

Duane's sister and some of the ladies in the church wanted to baby him. They meant well; they loved us and wanted to help. But, I just had a feeling if we babied him we would never see this thing through. I felt we had to be tough.

Feeling guilty one day, I called a lady in our church, Arlene Witt, who had had a long illness, and asked her if I was being too tough on Duane. She assured me that if we wanted to see great strides, we had to push hard.

Duane pushed himself, then the kids and I would come along and push just a little more. I look back now and wonder how he ever made it.

Another thing hard on Violet had to be my odd hours. I began going to bed at 8 p.m. even if she still had chores to do or even if the kids were still out. Keep in mind all of this went on over a period of seven years. Violet describes how hard it was:

> If the kids were out on dates, I would wait up for them. I would get upset at Duane for going to bed so early. I was tired, too, but I knew things had to get done, plus the kids needed to talk when they got in.
>
> When Mark got home from a date or being out with the youth group from church, he would pat the bed and want me to sit down and talk. Tired as I was, we did grow close and had some neat late-night conversations.
>
> I don't think the people outside of the immediate family knew the struggles that went on in the home. Once Duane's hair grew back and covered the scar, he would put forth his best effort in front of others. But there was no way for outsiders to know what great struggles we were still going through.

It's true. I remember that the healing would seem to be progressing so well, then I would have a setback. We could never figure why until we looked back later and realized there had been a lot of stress in my life at those particular times.

"There were a lot of good times and neat memories," says Patrece. "One thing that helped a lot was that my dad had such a good sense of humor. He could always laugh. Even when he made a mistake in his speaking, we would laugh about it. He knew that we weren't laughing at him, but we were laughing at what was funny in the situation."

Patrece recalls in particular a family vacation we took in a motor home. "We were swimming in a pool at a campground, and some people were making fun of my dad. My cousin and I got real upset. Yet my dad just let it roll off his back. He could laugh about it and make jokes.

"He had a way of making people feel comfortable about his situation. Even to this day, we can tell stories of ways that he pronounced different words that would come out really funny. Like the time he was trying to say 'candy bar,' and it came out 'candy beer.' "

I remember one time we were coming back from eastern Oregon. Violet and I had gotten into an argument, and she had stopped the car. Frustrated, I said, "Hey, you're better off without me," and I walked away. My purpose in walking was not to make a dramatic display. I actually wanted to walk off into oblivion.

Then I heard something behind me.

It was Mark. He was perhaps 15 or 16 years old by then. I didn't turn around, but I felt this arm around my shoulders. Then he said, "Dad, you're gonna make it. You're the best preacher I've ever heard. You're gonna make it."

Violet later told me how she dealt with the stress of our lives:

I used to imagine scenarios in which I would fake getting killed in an accident with the car, and leave the kids and Duane and start life over somewhere else. I know we were all under such terrible stress. I just wish we would have recognized it for what it was and gone to prayer more readily.

Once, two or three years after the surgery, Violet left me a note and said, "I'm leaving." It broke my heart. I just sobbed uncontrollably.

Now when your wife leaves you, and you're the pastor of the church, you can't call your church board and say, "My wife has left me." So I called my immediate superior in our denomination, R.E. Book. I sobbed to him, "Violet's left me."

He said, "I'll be right there." He and Ormal Chapin, a good friend and fellow minister of mine, drove from Salem, Oregon, which is about an hour away. In the meantime, Violet had felt terrible about what she had done and had come home. So, I had to tell her that he was coming because I had told him that she had left.

"I was so embarrassed," says my wife.

But he was so kind, so wise.

It was the best thing in the world that could have happened.

"Yes," agrees my wife. "Brother Book came and talked with us, and it was good. It was embarrassing to say the least. In fact, I still get embarrassed just thinking about it."

Brother Book had known me years before my surgery. He knew what a blowhard I could be. As my ministry had grown, it was one of those situations where the woman behind the scene doesn't get the credit. But a lot of credit goes to Violet because, like most men who succeed, I couldn't have done it without her.

Violet's love and faithfulness were amazing. I thank God for her and my family — and their loyalty to me.

I remember, too, that my in-laws, Ron and Ruth Miller, were such a blessing to Violet and me during this difficult time. We had brought them to Christ Center Church to be our senior citizens pastors and had turned to them many times for counsel. Such wisdom from such godly people. We were blessed.

I have wondered why the professionals who worked with me at the hospital never once mentioned getting family counseling. When a man has been in the hospital for two months and has a long recovery ahead, his family needs help.

I know we certainly did.

P O S T C A R D
T E N

Seizures

Just before I had been released from the hospital, one of my doctors had come to my room to explain to Violet and me that I would have to take two kinds of medicine to prevent seizures.

Seizures?

This possibility had not been presented to us! The doctor said that after the brain goes through a trauma such as my surgery, grand mal and petit mal seizures often follow.

We, of course, stood there dumbfounded as he wrote out a prescription for dilantin and Phenobarbital, saying they would help stave off both kinds of seizures.

Nothing happened for about nine months after I came home. Then one day, I went to get wood for our fireplace. When I got back to the house, Mark was home from school and helped me unload and stack the logs in the basement. We finished just in time for dinner. Then I told Violet that I needed to get a bath and go to bed since I was exhausted and could not keep going any longer.

I later learned that I had pushed myself so hard that the dilantin had worked itself out of my system.

Patrece, whose bedroom was on the top floor above our master bedroom, heard unusual noises and rushed out of her room to find her mom.

Patrece said, "Mom! Dad called out your name kinda funny." Because Violet had been having trouble getting Patrece to go to bed, she told her to quit making excuses to stay up and go back to bed.

But Patrece insisted, screaming, "Something's wrong!" as she ran past her mother. "I just know it."

Violet and Mark bounded down the stairs after her and found me in the middle of a massive seizure — what is called a grand mal. None of them had ever seen one before and thought I was dying.

Patrece ran out the front door to our neighbors screaming, "My daddy's dying, my daddy's dying." They dialed 911.

Meanwhile, Violet fell apart, and it was only Mark who kept his head about him. He told Violet to get my pajama bottoms, saying that I wouldn't want to be seen naked no matter what my condition.

Mark began praying for me.

By this time I had stopped jerking and was as stiff as a board. So, here was Violet trying to lift my dead weight, at least my bottom half, to pull my pajamas up over my hips, crying the whole time.

Mark called Pastor Greg and Roxanne. At that time they lived about 10 blocks away. They rushed over, getting to the house just as the paramedics arrived. An ambulance rushed me to the hospital and intravenously gave me dilantin sodium.

Violet got curious about the dilantin because the doctors hadn't explained anything about it — only that it warded off seizures. She asked the pharmacist for a pamphlet on dilantin and discovered that one of the side effects of this drug is dyslexia, a condition that confuses the brain so that reading is very difficult.

Well, Violet thought, that's all Duane needs! She began praying that day for us to have faith to go off the dilantin and for a complete healing from seizures.

Since my episode of feeling so depressed and wanting to end it all, Violet and I had been making it a practice to praise the Lord at home and elsewhere — not just in church.

I believe there is enormous power in praising God. In fact, I had taught our people at Christ Center that praise is a covenant that God made with his people. A covenant is an agreement between two parties, "You do this, and I will do that."

Before the operation, when I was preaching and teaching on praise and worship, I was quick to point out that Psalm 81 says that God established a praise pact with the children of Israel. If they kept this agreement, God promised them four things.

First, He promised to keep them from satanic oppression. Psalm 81:9 says, "You shall have no foreign god among you." As long as we praise the Lord we will never fall into false worship. How reassuring that the first provision of this pact is that He will be our protector from all satanic attack.

Second, their worship would be pure. Psalm 81:9

says, "You shall not bow down to an alien god." He and He alone can cleanse the impure motives from our lives and keep our worship Christ-centered, rather than church, self, or program-centered. As R.A. Torrey used to say, "He is Lord of all or not at all."

Third, God promised that they would have a personal relationship with Him. Psalm 81:10 says, "I am the Lord your God." How do we come into this relationship? After we have been born again, there isn't always that close relationship we are desiring. As you begin to praise God, something wonderful happens to your confidence in your relationship to God. You are aware that He is, in fact, what you are declaring, YOUR LORD! This strengthens our faith so we can walk in confidence, facing our trials, knowing we have a secure relationship with God.

The fourth promise was that they would be protected from their enemies. Psalm 81:14 says, "How quickly would I subdue their enemies and turn my hand against their foes!"

There is an old saying among preachers. "This is where the rubber meets the road." I believe the seizures were my enemy, so Violet and I began to praise God — though it wasn't easy.

David said in Psalm 34:1, "I will bless the Lord at all times; his praise shall be continually in my mouth." I knew that praising God was supposed to be the norm of God's creation. It's easy to praise God when things are going well for us.

I didn't have any trouble praising God when we had a record attendance at Christ Center or when the board raised my salary. But the Lord was testing what I believed and taught. Now was the time that we had to offer the sacrifice of praise.

I describe sacrificing a praise to God as "the joyful acceptance of the messed-up present as part of God's natural plan for my future."

Jeremiah 29:11 says, "For I know the plans I have for you, declares the Lord, plans to prosper you and not to harm you, plans to give you hope and a future."

When the sacrifice of praise is in the life of the tested believer, it is producing something of greatness—it is refining us.

In the smeltering of gold and the removing of the dross, the goldsmith knows the process is finished when he can see his face reflected in the purified golden liquid. We should not plead with God to change our situation but praise Him, knowing through this test people will see God.

The sacrifice of praise is an offering. It costs something.

In 1 Chronicles 21:24, King David said to Araunah, "No, I insist on paying the full price. I will not take for the Lord what is yours, or sacrifice a burnt offering that costs me nothing." It is giving over to God what seemingly is my personal happiness, health, wealth, life, and future.

Praising Him gave Violet and me new strength. I believe we warded off many seizures just by praising the Lord.

One day as we were crossing a busy public street, I stepped off the curb and said, "Violet, I feel funny." A weird sensation swept over me, and I knew something was about to erupt in my body.

Immediately, we just began praising the Lord, "Thank You, Jesus. Praise You, Jesus. We love You, Jesus. Thank You, Lord," both of us said together. And the feeling was gone, just as quickly as it had come.

Another time we were on a missionary trip to Japan and our plane had just landed. As we deboarded, I felt a seizure coming on and grabbed Violet's hand. She held on to me tightly as we walked through Narita International Airport, praising God out loud.

Regardless of where we were, we praised God with our voices whenever we needed to ward off an attack of the enemy.

Now, that's not to say that I didn't have any more seizures. All in all I had nine grand mal seizures, but they came after I had fallen asleep, so there was no way to know they were coming on.

By this time, through much prayer, Violet and I decided to step out in faith and go off the dilantin. We knew God was healing me, step by step, and that we couldn't see the complete results because of the side effects of the dilantin.

I had my last seizure when Violet wasn't there. It was so violent that I bit all the way through my tongue and thrashed around so much that my toes and fingers were bruised. I don't know if I hit the bedpost or what, but I had bruises all over my body.

When I arrived at the hospital, they filled me so full of dilantin that I didn't know if I was coming or going. I was so despondent. I felt let down.

Although I had tried so hard to trust God for healing, the seizure still happened.

I called my father the next day and said, "Dad, I'm a little bit discouraged. I had a grand mal last night."

By the way, my father is more than 80 years old now, but he still pastors a church and still preaches every Sunday.

"Well, son, let's pray," he said. And we prayed.

My father is a real prayer warrior. Later at a fellowship meeting, my father told the people, "My son has a physical need." My dad is of the old school. He doesn't let out any more information than necessary. But he had them pray — without giving the details of my problem.

Afterward, a man came to my dad and said, "Tell your son that God has healed him of seizures. Tell your son he will never have another seizure. God told me he was healed."

Dad had not said a thing about seizures.

I've never had another one.

Praise the Lord.

The Gethsemane Experience

That night in my office at home — when I was so low that I wanted to commit suicide — I was faced with a choice. It had nothing to do with the ability of God to heal, nothing to do with the ability of God to say, "Speak, My child." It had to do with my stubborn will.

Would I submit my will to God's holy will? Or would I follow Lucifer's evil example and rebel, pursuing my own foolish will?

We all, at one point or another, enter the garden plot called Gethsemane. It is disconcerting because it is filled with pain, sorrow, and trouble, and our emotions are tested to the very limit.

What is the purpose, we ask?

I'm not proposing to be an expert on Gethsemane, but I know a little bit about it because of the struggles that Violet and I have gone through, and also through a book I have been reading by Ray Beeson called, *That I May Know Him,* God is teaching us something that I want to impart to you.

Jesus, the Son of God, had his own Gethsemane. Matthew 26:36-39 says, "Then Jesus went with his disciples to a place called Gethsemane, and he said to them, 'Sit here while I go over there and pray.' He took Peter and the two sons of Zebedee along with him, and he began to be sorrowful and troubled. Then he said to them, 'My soul is overwhelmed with sorrow to the point of death. Stay here and keep watch with me.' Going a little farther, he fell with his face to the ground and prayed, 'My Father, if it is possible, may this cup be taken from me. Yet not as I will, but as you will.' "

It is important for us to realize that when we go through a Gethsemane experience, the will of God is the crucial issue involved. Not our healing, not our finances, not the bringing back to us what is lost, but the will of God. All these things may come to us in time, but only according to God's will.

It is in the Gethsemanes of our lives that we find out where our wills are in relationship to the will of God. Only a Gethsemane experience would cause a person to say, "I seek not to please myself, but Him who sent me." That very statement from the Lord is applicable to us.

God made it so clear to me, while I was holding the gun in my hand, that two opposing wills constantly confront one another in the universe: the will of God and the will of Satan.

The Holy Spirit showed me the importance of what they were fighting for. They weren't fighting for Portland, Oregon. They weren't fighting over the United States or the world. They were fighting for each individual soul.

Combat is waged in the heavens for each one of us. The consequences of rebelling against God and joining Satan's rebellion are death, defilement, and destruction.

I actually sensed the voice of the enemy laughing in my ears: "Where's your God? You've preached all your life that God will never leave you or forsake you. Where's your God? He's only a figment of your imagination."

On the other hand, the rewards of submitting to the will of God is always life, liberty, and laughter.

The Holy Spirit brought to mind the words of my godly father when he sensed the call of God was on my life. He took me aside and said, "Son, in all your learning, remember this, the Holy Spirit is a gentleman, and He will not cross the threshold of your will."

I knew Dad was right. I wouldn't be forced to surrender my will to God. It had to be my choice. Although I couldn't see the future. I had to trust that God knew what He was doing in my life.

God is not interested in violating the human will. He will not force us to surrender our wills to His will, but He will allow us to be pressed to the point where we are compelled to look closely at the consequences of the decisions we make.

God is not trying to change us to where we will be miserable when we submit to His will. The amazing thing to me was that the Lord didn't take me by the nape of the neck and say, "I can't believe you, Duane Parrish. After all I've been to you, and you're acting this way!" Just a gentle voice came to me and said, "Son, have I ever let you down? Can't you trust Me?"

That's when I threw the gun down to the floor and lifted my hands up. I said, "God, forgive me for my rotten attitude."

The psalmist David said, "I delight to do your will." There's a delighting process in doing the will of God.

Romans 8:31 says, "What shall we then say to these things. If God be for us, who can be against us?" Everything God allows to touch our lives is for our good, not for our demise.

What comes out of the Gethsemane experience? A depth of seeing God. Job 42:5 says, "My ears had heard of you but now my eyes have seen you. Therefore I despise myself and repent in dust and ashes."

After I threw the gun down and asked God to forgive me for my rotten attitude, the Lord revealed what He saw in my life. He showed me things that nobody else could have told me — and I listened. God revealed my heart, full of pride, full of self-centeredness, full of ego. It almost made me sick to see what God saw.

I said, "God, I'm sorry. Forgive me. Take those things away from me. I don't want to be proud. I don't want to boast. I want to be your servant."

It was only after we went through our Gethsemane that I saw the Lord.

My eyes were opened. I saw how much evil was in me. I saw how much I needed purged out of my life. And then I saw myself, as if I were crawling upon a potter's wheel, and I said, "God, if You have to break me into a million pieces, that's okay.

"But don't take Your spirit from me."

P O S T C A R D
T W E L V E

A New Leaf

I was determined to turn over a new leaf, or a new page in my life. I thought, *Hey, God had His chance to take me home, but He chose to leave me here. I don't know for what purpose, but I am going to be sensitive to the Lord and have Him work out that purpose in my life — and be content.*

I began to go on walks every morning, and on these walks some incredible things happened. For the first time in my life I had time to notice businesses, people, and places that I had never looked at before.

A stained glass shop near our home caught my eye one day. In all the years I had lived there, I had never gone inside. I went in, smiled at the owner, took my hat off, pointed at the scar on my head, and began to communicate as best I could. The owner was very gracious.

I also went into the local bakery at Beaverton and started to visit with the employees there.

Several places of business became regular stops on my daily walks. As I began to build relationships, some of my new-found friends were converted to Christ and are now serving the Lord. So, I want you to know that even a brain-damaged guy who plays with a Speak and Spell can win people to Jesus.

About nine or ten months after my surgery, I thought it was time to have a meeting with the church board. I hadn't really approached anybody in the church before this time about church business or the future.

Violet and I had kept mostly to ourselves, staying in the house because of my severe depression.

After the Lord dealt with me so powerfully the night I almost killed myself and the depression departed, I thought it was time to talk to the church board.

I began to feel it wasn't fair for the board to have to make this decision of what to do with a pastor who couldn't talk, read, or write. Although I was beginning to make progress on all three fronts, I wasn't there, yet.

When I called the board together, I knew that I had to resign my position as pastor.

Once, earlier in my ministry, I had a terrible experience with the board of a church we had pastored.

The night of the board meeting I had taken Violet to the hospital. She was to have a Cesarean section the next day for the birth of our daughter, Patrece. Before I left, I told her I would be by after the meeting to say goodnight.

During the meeting, one of the members stood up and said, "We are asking for your resignation."

"Why would you ask for my resignation?" I had

exclaimed, confused by this sudden rejection. I couldn't understand it since the church had been growing and, in fact, we were breaking attendance records. We were also well thought-of in the church community.

"We don't like you," the board member said.

I pulled myself together and called their attention to their own constitution and by-laws, noting that they had no cause for any action against me. Their by-laws said that the preacher could only be fired on moral or doctrinal grounds or if a two-thirds majority of the congregation approved the firing in a congregational meeting.

Then, I said, "I kindly would thank you to turn out the lights when you're through. I'm leaving. I have a wife in the hospital."

I acted very bold and very brave, but when I got outside it was as if a knife had pierced my heart. My leadership had been rejected.

Since they could not get a two-thirds vote to kick me out, I stayed around for about three months, and then we finally left.

How could they act like that? Because they are human — just as we all are. Because none of us are sinless, except for the Lord, we must accept the reality that offenses come to the household of faith. Why? It is by those very offenses we are able to practice forgiveness and thereby grow up into the measure of Christ.

N.D. Davidson, my former superintendent, was fond of reciting this little poem:

> To live with the saints in Heaven
> will be bliss and glory.
> To live with the saints here on earth
> is quite a different story.

A country songwriter put the same thought a different way with the line, "I beg your pardon, I never promised you a rose garden."

When we give our hearts to the Lord, our eternal salvation does not exclude us from testings and trials. Many times God tests what we have ingested into our spirits.

Things happen to us that produce pain. Misconduct by the opposite sex, child molestation, divorce, harsh words, church splits, and so many other offenses cause great heartache. I'm confident as you read this that the Holy Spirit will reveal wounds of your own that need to be dealt with as well.

The apostle Paul addressed this issue when he wrote in Ephesians 3:14-19 that he prayed before the Father that out of His glorious riches He would strengthen us with power through His spirit in our inner being, so that Jesus Christ may dwell in our hearts through faith. He wrote that he also prayed that we, being rooted and established in love, might have power, together with all the saints, to grasp how wide and long and high and deep is the love of Christ our Lord, and to know this love that surpasses knowledge — that we may be filled to the measure of all the fullness of God.

America's War Between the States left a tragic aftermath of bitterness, hatred, and resentment — particularly in the vanquished South. The wounds inflicted were deep and painful. Though the guns finally fell silent, the anger lived on.

Many could not forget or forgive what had been done. The resentment was passed on from generation to generation.

One man who refused to participate in or condone

this terrible harvest of bitterness was the South's great hero, Gen. Robert E. Lee. In word and in deed, Lee urged reconciliation between the North and the South. He knew the war was over and that the future of the nation demanded a new attitude for a new day. To the day of his death, he was never heard to speak an unkind word about those who had been his former enemies.

On one occasion, a lady in Lexington, Virginia, showed him the scarred remains of a tree in her yard. During a raid all the limbs had been shot off by Yankee artillery. Thinking the general would share her feelings of outrage, she waited expectantly for him to comment.

Finally, Lee spoke, "Cut it down, my dear madam, and forget it."

In many ways that is good advice for us. Let us therefore cut down and forget.

Let me take you back to the injury that I suffered from my first board. When I did resign, I told God that I would never work with a board again. I got bitter in my spirit, and I ran for three years. Then I received a call to pastor the church in Beaverton.

I said to myself, *Okay, but I won't get close to my board members.*

On the nights of the board meetings I often became sick. Anxiety would sweep over me. Sometimes I even lost my supper out of fear that this board would ask me to resign as well. I was good at hiding my feelings, but they remained anyway.

Since I am a people person, I did get close to my board members anyway. I trusted them and depended upon their input and advice.

So I was approaching my resignation from Christ Center Church with the attitude that I loved this board, I loved this church, and I wasn't going to put them in a situation to come to me and ask me to resign.

The meeting was held in one of the board member's home. I got up, remembering that other traumatic meeting. *This is the last board meeting that I will have with my friends,* I thought.

As I choked back the tears, I said, "Men." And I prayed that God would give me a clarity of speech.

I chose my words carefully since it was still very difficult for most people to understand me. God gave me a clarity of speech that evening, so slowly I said, "I'm going to resign as your pastor."

Immediately one of the board members got up and asked, "Is God telling you to resign?"

Well, I couldn't say that God was telling me to resign. I was doing this because I didn't want the board to have to worry about me. I said, "No, but ...."

He said, "Pastor, I don't want to know why or what led you to say you are going to resign. I just want to know if God is speaking."

He said to the other members, "I want to know. This is the most important decision that we'll ever have to make. Has God been speaking to you whether Pastor is supposed to resign or not?"

I had a seven-man board, and seven "no's" came in. The board member turned back to me and said, "There you have it. You are our pastor." Then, they gave me a year and a half off — with a raise in pay.

Suddenly, I knew there was something I had to do. Something I had said I would never do. But, inside my heart, the Lord was prompting me to obey Him. I said to my associate pastor, "Greg, would you get a basin of water and a towel? Men, I want to wash your feet."

Although I had heard my father talk about participating in this very humbling ceremony, I didn't know exactly how to go about it. I figured that I wasn't supposed to scrub but just symbolically to pour water all over their feet, so that's what I did.

As I knelt beside each man's feet, I said, "I want to be God's servant and your servant."

I washed all of their feet and then they said, "Pastor? Would you take off your shoes and socks? We want to wash your feet."

For a moment, I knew I wasn't worthy and almost refused. The Lord was dealing with me, and He said, "What about that first church board? What about that root of bitterness that has sprung up in your heart? Would you be willing to forgive the first board?"

I said, "Yes, I would."

A few weeks later, knowing that the first church I pastored was having special meetings, I decided to attend. It didn't dawn on me that some of the board members might have moved away. That night, however, I think every board member was present in the service. In fact, some who had moved away had come to visit the church.

I gathered them around and I said, "Would you forgive me for the bitterness that I have had in my heart toward you?"

They said, "Yes, providing you will forgive us." And we embraced.

There was an inner healing that took place in my life that night.

I forgave those men.

And they forgave me.

There is truly great power in forgiveness.

The Cussing Preacher

I kept going to physical rehabilitation classes and doing what the therapists said to do. My family was also helping me with my exercises, and I worked constantly with my Speak and Spell.

Improvement came slowly, but we continued to attend church. In fact, I sometimes tried to participate in the services.

When I began to speak in front of the congregation and tried to express myself, the words would come out all wrong. I said bad words.

I was playing a saxophone duet with one of my board members, Everett Loughridge. The song was called

"Mansions Can't Be Bought in Heaven."

The melody sounded a lot like the song made popular by Elvis Presley, "Old Shep Was My Dog." I thought to myself, as we were playing, "I forgot to announce the title of this song."

Now you have to understand, I was speaking semi-okay if I took things slow. But when I was rushed or got excited, watch out!

As the song ended, I quickly stepped to the mike and said, "In case you were wondering, that song was not "Old #$&@." I just stopped talking, I was so embarrassed.

I actually said "the S word" as clear as a bell.

One of my deacons asked, "Did he say what I think he said?"

Now that I look back, it was funny. But at the time I was very embarrassed to be using four letter words in church.

Maybe that's why I overheard our greeters at the front door sharing with every newcomer what had happened to their pastor. I get a chuckle when I think about it.

I remember one time going over to my associate pastor's apartment building for a swim in their pool. It was crowded with sunbathers.

Greg, Roxanne, Violet, and I were the only ones actually in the water. I swam underwater and came up at the other end of the pool and said something quite loud to them.

Somehow I got excited, so it came out all garbled. The sunbathers all stared. The people sitting around the pool looked at me very strangely, so I thought real quick and announced to everybody rather haltingly, "Uh, how you say in English?"

Whew — got out of that one.

Oh, you should have heard me. I would try so hard, but it came out just totally garbled. Since I was never bashful, I would try anything the therapist asked — no matter how terrible it sounded. I was very fortunate through all of this because I did manage to keep my sense of humor.

After I got through the depression stage, I even tried to be funny at times. One time the therapist held up a stop sign and instead of saying, "Stop," which was hard for me to pronounce, I just said, "Alto," which is Spanish for stop.

She just cracked up. She could not believe how my mind was working. I knew that I could not say the "st" consonant blend. I knew that "stop" had an "st," so I thought up a way to get out of my predicament.

I found out that I was good at synonyms. I would think of things that were unbelievable sometimes. If I knew I couldn't say the word they were asking for, I would think of a word with the same meaning. It was fun.

As a matter of fact, the therapist came to church several times because she was so impressed with my progress. My male nurse also visited our church. It blessed me to know I was able to sow the Word of God in the lives of those who dealt with me the most at the hospital — and there were conversions.

At times, people thought I was drunk. I can't tell you how many telephone operators hung up on me because they thought I'd had one too many drinks.

When I came under pressure, what progress I had made often dissipated. I remember one incident in particular having to do with Marley Anderson. He was the pastor of the local Nazarene church.

Before my surgery, whenever I saw Marley in a restaurant or other public places, I would go up to him, extend my hand, and say, "How are you doing? How are things at the church?" I'm sure that he took notice of my concern, but we never got together.

After my surgery, and before I could drive my car, I was out walking one day near the Nazarene church, which was about three blocks from my house. Suddenly, the Lord said, "Go in and have Marley pray for you."

So I went into the church office and said to the secretary, "I'm here to see Marley Anderson." I was just barely able to pronounce my words and must have sounded like I was drunk.

She said, "I don't know if he can see you, let me see."

I overheard her saying, "There is a man here to see you. He appears to be drunk, and he wants you to pray for him."

So Marley graciously opened his door to this drunk man, and he saw it was me. He sat back with a start in his chair and exclaimed, "Duane, what has happened?"

I bent my head down and said, "I have had brain surgery. I'm having difficulty talking and writing and reading. I felt like you could pray for me."

Well, he did, and that was the beginning of a fruitful relationship with him and his church. As the time progressed and I got better and better, I remember Marley saying to me, "Duane, we should have a joint service with Christ Center and Beaverton Nazarene."

I said, "Okay."

"You can give your testimony."

By this time I had progressed to the point where I was able to give my testimony in public meetings, so we set a date for the service.

When the time came, the two congregations gathered at Marley's church. As usual I had brought along my saxophone. In fact, the first thing that came back to me after the surgery was the ability to worship the Lord with my instrument.

Every Sunday, I would play the hymns and the choruses as the congregation of our church sang. Tears would course down my cheeks as I sang with them in my mind, getting lost in the spirit.

So I had brought my saxophone to the Nazarene church and was putting it together. As I stuck the reed on the mouthpiece, Marley came to me and said, "We don't allow saxophones in our church."

Knowing Marley to be a great kidder, I ventured out and said, "This saxophone is okay because it's been sanctified."

He laughed and said, "I'm just kidding."

We had a great relationship.

One Sunday morning I felt God speak to my heart about helping Marley's church with their building program. At the next board meeting of our church, I said to the men, "God, is talking to me, and I want your approval. I would like to take the Sunday morning offering and give it in its entirety to the Nazarene church to help them in their building program."

When I informed Marley what I was going to do, he said, "You can't do that."

I said, "Are you arguing with God? God told me to do this and my board has agreed, so we are going to do it."

It was wonderful to have a small part in helping them build their church. Marley and I have been close friends ever since.

One day Marley told me about the founding father of the organization of the Nazarenes, Uncle Bud Robinson. He explained that Robinson talked with a lisp and had grand mal seizures while in the pulpit. This dear man, who was somewhat handicapped, was fond of saying, "God doesn't need much of a man if he can have all of that man."

That inspired me. "God you've got everything that I have. My warts and all."

One day, when I was so discouraged, I was driving to Portland and passed by the First Assembly of God there, where my friend, David Elms, was the pastor.

I said to myself, "I need him to pray for me." So I turned into the parking lot and walked into the church office.

After introducing myself to the receptionist, I asked, "Is the pastor here?"

She said, "Yes, he is, but he is in a staff meeting. He can't see you."

That kind of irritated me. I was in no mood for negotiations with a receptionist, so I said, "Yeah, he will see me."

I knew where the staff meetings were held, so I just barged in — with her protesting behind me. I opened the door, and there was the pastor with his large staff, following a formal agenda.

Dave said, "Hi, Duane. What brings you here?"

I said, "Dave, I need somebody to pray with me."

I'll never forget what happened. Pastor Dave pulled up a chair and told me to sit in the middle of their circle. They reached their hands out to me and touched me. They didn't preach to me or say, "Now the Word of God says this and so on." They just loved me and prayed for me and wept with me.

After about 10 or 15 minutes of praying, I thanked them, went out, saluted the receptionist who had said I couldn't go in, and was encouraged in my soul. The touch of their hands upon my shoulder meant everything in the world to me. I knew that I had brothers in the ministry who were standing by me in my affliction. They didn't have any counsel to give me, just love.

Although I am unable to list them all here, I want you to know that it was God's gift of godly friends who helped me through some of my most difficult times.

Over a year after my surgery, I started to give little sermonettes from the pulpit and say the offertory prayer or make announcements. As the months progressed, I was in the pulpit and before the congregation more and more.

Another thing that bothered me was that my spelling was so atrocious. I talked to the Lord about this and said, "God, You have been so good to give me back my speech and my writing. Could You help me on my spelling?"

He answered, "You couldn't spell before!"

An He wuzz rite.

Get the Wesson Oil

I love to hunt. So about a year after my surgery, I began thinking about going on an elk hunting trip. I bounced the idea off one of my deacons, and he was enthusiastic.

We decided to get together for lunch at a nice restaurant in Portland on the Columbia River to discuss our plans. As Violet and I were on our way to pick up his wife, I noticed a man standing alongside the road in a jogging outfit. Instead of running, he was hitchhiking.

I remember thinking it odd that he had on matching jogging pants and jacket and shoes and even a matching cap, but there he was — thumbing for a ride.

I was driving and said to Violet, "We have got to pick him up."

She looked at me in surprise "What?" she asked. She knew I didn't pick up hitchhikers. It's too dangerous these days. But I was insistent, and I slammed on the brakes.

She opened the door and the stranger got into the back seat. Thoughts flashed through my mind, *What if he's a robber? What if he is a criminal who has just escaped? Does he look like Charles Manson?*

I adjusted my rear-view mirror so I could watch him. *If he pulls a gun or tries to do anything out of the ordinary, I will accelerate quickly, then slam on the brakes, throwing him forward so I can grab his gun and be the hero.* So I got that all straight in my mind.

Then he began to speak. "It's nice to have you pick me up," he said. "I'm the pastor of the Lutheran church near here. I thought I would jog as far as Farmington, but got tired and started thumbing a ride."

The church he pastored was about three blocks from mine. I got excited. "You are? Ah, ah — You are?" I stammered in speech that was even more garbled than usual. "I'm — I'm — I'm a p-p-pastor, too!"

In the rearview mirror, I watched his face as his eyes got big. I could see that he doubted I could be any kind of preacher. I knew what was going on in his head. *What have I gotten myself into?*

Violet said, "This is Duane Parrish, pastor of Christ Center, here in Beaverton. Maybe you heard that he has gone through brain surgery?"

I stepped in. "Well, p-p-p-p-pastor!" I exclaimed, "you ah, ah, ah, can have y-y-your p-p-p-p-p-people ah, ah, pray for me."

"I will do that," he responded. "Listen, I was jogging out to a retired Lutheran pastor's place in Farmington. If you want to drive me out that far — he has the gift of healing. Do you have time to let him pray for you?"

"Sure," I exclaimed. So we went out to the retired Lutheran pastor's place. I will never forget the scene.

This retired Lutheran minister met us at the driveway. He wore overalls and a red flannel shirt and had his thumbs in his suspenders.

After welcoming us warmly, we went inside the house, and our hitchhiker introduced me as a neighboring pastor who had just gone through brain surgery. He said I needed to have prayer because I was continuing to struggle with speaking, writing, and reading.

He said, "Oh, we can do that. We'll be glad to pray for you." He called to his wife, "Honey, do we have any olive oil?"

She looked in the cupboard and began to search. As we talked, I could hear the sounds of bottles clinking and cans being pushed around the shelves, then the refrigerator opening, then closing, then opening again.

She looked up after a couple of minutes and said, "No, we don't."

I spoke up and said, "Get the Wesson Oil!" So she brought a king size bottle of cooking oil.

What came next was an experience that followed what the Bible calls "anointing with oil" — but which was totally different than anything we ever did in our church. I was accustomed to taking the olive oil and placing the base of the bottle on the thumb with the pointer finger placed on the top.

Growing up, I had watched my dad as he tipped the

bottle to get oil on his pointer finger. Then, automatically, the little finger would point right toward heaven. Then he would search for a place on the person's forehead that didn't have any hair. On some people that was easy because the waves were gone and only the beach remained!

I was curious as to how this retired Lutheran pastor with the gift of healing would anoint me. His wife took off the lid of that king size bottle of cooking oil as he formed a cup with his hands. Then, she poured and poured and poured.

When he nodded to her, she stopped pouring. I watched astonished as the minister scrubbed the oil he held in his hands all over his knuckles, his wrists, his palms — totally saturating his hands.

Then he came toward me, and I thought, *Uh-oh, I'm going to be anointed.* All I could think about was Psalm 133:2, which describes anointing oil "that ran down upon the beard, even Aaron's beard; that went down to the skirts of his garments."

Then this dear man stopped and said, "Before we anoint you, let's praise God." So he lifted his hands, and we did, too.

I watched as the oil ran down his arms and dripped off his elbows onto his shirt — but he was oblivious to it as he praised the Lord, thanking God for who He is. I could not help but join in.

Then he came toward me and put his hands on my face, on my neck, on my hair, and he said, "Dear Jesus, we bring to You —" he paused and asked me, "What's your name?"

I said, "Duane."

"We bring to You Duane, and he has this problem.

Now You, God, can heal his problem and restore this brain, in Jesus name. Amen."

I went into that place with the dry look and showed up for lunch with my deacon and his wife with a very greasy look. However, I would not have traded that experience for anything. It truly was a blessing from God. Also out of that episode came my first sermon since my surgery.

Since my reading and writing were still poor, it took me a long time to prepare for my message. Studying the Bible and writing out my notes was tedious task, but I was determined.

I wanted to proclaim what a great God we have. I wanted my first sermon to be dramatic, powerful, and inspiring. I wanted everybody to have a powerful experience and renew their relationship with God in a rich and wonderful way. I wanted everything to be just right.

I even invited my male nurse and my speech therapist, and they were there.

I was very nervous. What would the people think of a slow-talking, inarticulate preacher? Was I doing this too soon? Could I get the people to understand what was on my heart? I turned to look at myself in the office mirror and had mixed feelings.

I was so glad to be back in the pulpit once again, but also I was afraid.

My brother, Richard Parrish, from Phoenix, Arizona, came, too. I asked him to stand with me in the pulpit and do the reading of the Scriptures since reading was still a very slow process for me.

But this wasn't the only reason I wanted him to stand there beside me. I knew my brother's 6-foot-3 frame would make me feel more secure — and if I couldn't pull the sermon off, I knew he was an excellent communicator. He could finish if I broke down.

We walked to the platform, and Richard asked everyone to turn to 1 Corinthians 2:1-5. As he began to read, I started to cry for joy, just at the thought that God was returning me to the pulpit.

I listened to Rich read the words of Paul: "And I, brethren, when I came to you, came not with excellency of speech or of wisdom, declaring unto you the testimony of God. For I determined not to know any thing among you, save Jesus Christ, and him crucified" (1 Cor. 2:1-2).

Then, I began to speak.

I pointed out that Paul in this passage shows us what made his ministry so effective. It was none other than the anointing of God. I noted that there are three inter-related words that make up the anointing.

Chrio — to anoint.

Christos — the anointed one.

Chrisma — the anointing or the unction.

It is God who anoints; He is the anointer. The nearer we get to Him, the more the anointing flows. That is why I believe that if we are going to be used of God, we have got to get next to God. We have got to learn of His character and ways. We have got to learn that His ways are not our ways, His thoughts are not our thoughts, and that He, indeed, has a greater plan than we could ever know.

It is Christ, the anointed one, that we proclaim. We have got to get next to the Son, Jesus. We have to have an intimate relationship with Him. We have got to have that fellowship, unbroken, with Him. We can have the most prestigious programs, but if we don't proclaim Jesus Christ under the anointing, the church becomes a dinner club.

It is the Holy Spirit that dispenses the anointing. We have got to get next to the Holy Spirit. He has got to fill our lives so that the sweetness of the Holy Spirit is coming out. It is the Holy Spirit that gives unction to fulfill the plans that God has given to us while we are near to Him.

Paul's whole ministry was built upon "-ter, -ted, and -ting" — the Anoin-ter, the Anoin-ted, and the Anoin-ting. The Lord is calling the body of Christ to be anointed in all of our ways.

That was my first sermon.

It may not show up in classic literature alongside Jonathan Edwards' *Sinners in the Hands of an Angry God* or compiled with the best of Charles Wesley, Smith Wigglesworth, or Billy Graham.

However, it was a start.

God Gives a Voice

About two years after my surgery, I was in the church office and the phone rang. My secretary got it and said, "Pastor, it's for you. It's your nurse."

So I picked up the phone and asked, "Karen, what's going on?"

She said, "Duane, we have a young teenage boy here who has gone through a similar surgery like yours, an AV malformation of the brain. He's not doing too well. We can't control him. He's violently angry. I thought you could talk to him."

I said, "I will be right up."

But on the way to the hospital, I said, "God, I don't know what to tell him; You will have to speak through me."

I walked into the boy's hospital room and saw food

on the wall where he had thrown it. The chaotic condition caused by the angry teenager was obvious.

The Spirit of God came upon me, and I knelt by the boy's bed. I said, "I understand you went through a brain operation similar to mine."

I tilted my head so he could put his fingers in the three holes about a half inch deep. As he did this, I said, "Let me tell you what Jesus did in my life when I yielded myself to Him."

Step by step I was able to tell him about the love of Christ and watched as the young man's anger dissipated.

I saw Karen, his nurse, standing in the corner of the room shaking her head in disbelief.

When we got out in the hall, I asked, "Karen, what were you shaking your head for?"

She said, "Duane, I don't know about you, but it seems to me you can do more good than most doctors can."

I said, "Not true. It's not me. It's the Lord Jesus Christ. I just share what He's done in my life. He has given me a voice in more ways than one."

Romans 8:28 is a fitting Scripture for me. In fact, I think it is a capstone in my life.

All Scripture is given for us as believers, but we need to have foundational Scriptures that speak directly to us specifically. Then, when we go through trials and testings, the Holy Spirit will cause those Scriptures to come into focus.

I believe that the apostle Paul is writing to us in Romans 8:28 words that will give us hope and give us a foundation to stand on when our testing times come.

You say, "But I'm not going to be tested."

All Christians go through testings. God didn't save us to give us a bed of roses. He saved us to put His Word in us, His Grace in us, and His love in us so that we can be His witnesses here on this earth.

What He has put in, He tests at periodic stages in our lives. I am thankful God does not test us all of our lives. We couldn't stand that.

In my darkest hours, when I thought the Lord had forsaken me, this Scripture came to my mind. "And we know that in all things God works for the good of those who love him, who have been called according to his purpose. For those God foreknew he also predestined to be conformed to the likeness of his Son, that he might be the firstborn among many brothers" (Rom. 8:28;NIV).

It was a long, hard battle. But through it all, God was there, every second, every minute, every hour of the day. There were times that I couldn't feel His presence, but I knew He was there.

I recalled what God said to Joshua. "No one shall be able to stand up against you all the days of your life. As I was with Moses, so I will be with you; I will never leave you nor forsake you" (Josh. 1:5;NIV).

I was beginning to learn that faith is a journey, not a destination.

When you are going through a test and you yield yourself to the unseen God, knowing that He does all things well, knowing that He has you in His hands, knowing that He is aware of your situation and your circumstance, it has a way of refining our reverence for the Lord.

There's a beautiful story in Genesis 22 of Abraham and Isaac. In verse 1, Abraham was tested by God. In verse 2, God told Abraham to offer up his son Isaac on the altar.

In verse 3, Abraham obeyed and started out on his journey.

In verse 7, Isaac said to his father, "I see the fire in the firepan, the wood on the donkey, but where is the burnt offering?"

In verse 8, Abraham answered the son and said, "God will provide."

Have you ever been to that place in your testing where you knew that God was the One who had to supply because it was beyond you to supply what you needed?

Well, Abraham and Isaac built the altar, and the time came to obey. Abraham took his knife, raised it, and was about to slay his son. Then he heard from heaven, "Don't lay a hand on that boy. Don't do anything to him. Now I know that you fear Me, because you have not withheld from Me your only son."

Abraham took the most precious thing in his life and was willing to give it to the Lord if that's what He wanted.

There comes a time when God tests us on the most important things in our lives. He tested me. He will test you.

When I thought I would never speak again, when I thought I could not communicate God's Word to the people again, I realized that God was asking for one of the dearest things to me. When I was willing to give my communicative abilities to the Lord, He put a reverence in my heart for the things of God.

"Abraham looked up and there in a thicket he saw a ram caught by its horns. He went over and took the ram and sacrificed it as a burnt offering instead of his son. So Abraham called that place The Lord Will Provide . . ." (Gen. 22:13-14;NIV).

I never approach a service without getting down

on my knees and saying, "God I need You, Oh, how I need You in this service tonight. Minister to these people through me. Let Your anointing fall."

We need that reverence in our hearts for God. Society and the Church have downplayed the importance of reverence.

Abraham is a type of God, and Isaac is a type of Jesus. Jesus was sent to the world, by God, to be a sacrifice for mankind. In that sacrifice was made provision for all we will ever need. God provided for our salvation, for our healing, for our miracles, and for our counseling. For everything that touches our lives, the provision is found in Christ. The Lord has provided, is providing, and will provide.

Little by little, day by day, my communication skills started coming back to me. Now I have been released from pastoring — by God and Christ Center — to fulfill a calling that is now on my heart: evangelism. I travel approximately 50 weeks out of the year giving my testimony and telling hurting people that they are destined to overcome.

My physical condition is getting better and better all the time. The doctors can't understand how I have come as far as I have, but they didn't know my doctor — Dr. Jesus.

With each passing day, I recognize how unworthy I am, but He has made me worthy and given me a voice.

God's Delays

I was fortunate to be surrounded by many faithful and selfless people during my recovery period — people who made a big difference and without whom my life would not be the same today.

About a year before my surgery, the Lord sent me a prayer partner, a Baptist preacher.

He was pastoring a neighboring church and one day went to check on an elderly couple from his congregation who lived across the street from Christ Center Church. When he didn't get any answer, this pastor came into my office and introduced himself.

"I'm Carl Blanchard, the pastor of Allen Avenue Baptist Church. The couple across the street go to my church, and they are elderly. Would you keep an eye on that house?"

We began to talk, and I said that I had been praying that the Lord would send me a prayer partner. He surprised me by saying, "I have been praying for a prayer partner, too."

God spoke to my heart and said, *Well, here is the prayer partner you asked Me to send you.*

Without answering aloud, I responded, *God, he doesn't believe the same way that I believe. He's a Baptist and doesn't believe in being spirit-filled. He doesn't speak in tongues.*

God said, *But he can pray.*

So, I blurted out, "Would you be my prayer partner?"

Carl said, "I would love to."

The first time we met together to pray, I thought, *If we are going to have a successful relationship in this prayer partnership, then we are going to have to establish some ground rules.*

I figured there were two theological issues that separated us — speaking in tongues and the Baptist doctrine of eternal security.

So, I told him, "Carl, you believe in once saved, always saved. I don't. Instead, I believe it is possible to lose your salvation.

"I also believe in speaking in tongues, and you don't. Can we put these two doctrinal issues on the shelf? Let's pull them down only when you want to know about speaking in tongues, or if I need to understand why you believe in eternal security."

He agreed.

Through the years, Carl has grown so dear to my heart. After my surgery, my assistant pastor, Greg Hickman, was filling the pulpit on Sunday mornings and nights.

However, I was in search of a Wednesday night Bible teacher. Carl had just resigned his church to go back to college to get his doctorate so I asked him to teach for me on Wednesday nights.

He said, "But I'm not a Pentecostal."

"Did I ask you to come on Wednesday night to speak in tongues? No, I need you to teach my Bible class for me."

Well, he did a great job.

That class grew and grew. Carl taught us for a year out of the Gospel of John, going through the entire book.

One day, he told me that he had come to John 10:29, which says, "No man is able to pluck them out of my Father's hand." He said that the Baptist interpretation is that it is impossible for a Christian to fall from grace.

I gave him the liberty of interpreting the Scripture the way he believed. He told the class his view of eternal security, and then he turned it over to me.

I remember that I was praying — oh, how I was praying. I said, "God, You said if we lacked wisdom we should seek it from You."

Immediately, I received what I believe was an inspiration. I turned to the class and stammered, "Both Carl and I believe in the insecurity of the unbeliever."

Everyone laughed and clapped their hands.

In the months that followed, Carl was a tremendous help to me in understanding the ways of God. In fact, he gave me a sermon that totally revolutionized my life. It helped me understand God's delays — the times when we ask the Lord for something, and it doesn't happen immediately.

Carl told me it's easy to develop a "vending machine" type of prayer life.

I understand all about vending machines.

Today, whenever my ministry takes me out of town, I stay in motels. When I get hungry for a snack, I go down to the vending machines, put my money in, punch "A-1," and watch the machine drop a high-cholesterol bag of chips.

It's easy to view God as a vending machine.

We get on our knees, ask for what we want, then look around to see where it is.

But God is not a vending machine. He has a master plan for us — and sometimes what we see as a need, He does not.

We may think that we just have to have that new job in the big city. However, when we don't get it, that doesn't mean that God ignored us. He may know that we aren't ready yet for that dream. He may have something better for us somewhere else.

Do you remember Jesus' friend Lazarus, the brother of Mary and Martha? The story told about him in John 11 demonstrates how God's delays are always deliberate and never accidental.

We must come to grips with the fact that when we pray sincere prayers and God doesn't answer the way we want Him to answer, it's not accidental at all.

Jesus received word that Lazarus was sick in John 11:3. However, the Lord did not immediately head for their home in Bethany. Jesus deliberately delayed. When He heard that Lazarus was sick, he stayed where he was two more days. Then He said to His disciples, "Let us go."

For no apparent reason, He delayed. It wasn't that He couldn't get a plane reservation or that the trains and buses were not moving. It was a short distance from where He was to where Lazarus lived. Nevertheless, He delayed.

To serve a God who has the capacity to accidentally forget me and my situation would be to serve no god at all. But my God's delays are always with my best interests in mind.

Jesus knew full well, in His divine wisdom, the final result.

I believe that when God heard my 14-year-old Mark's prayer that day in the hospital, He did not ignore my boy's fervent prayer nor disregard my son's young faith.

He heard Mark, but God has his own timetable.

Jesus knew His friend Lazarus was going to die. The Lord took his time getting to Lazarus' bedside, actually let him die, then used his death to demonstrate God's incredible power.

After the Disciples saw Lazarus step forth from the tomb after being dead several days, they no longer had any doubt as to who they were following.

Jesus was the Lord.

He was the fulfillment of prophecies.

He was the Messiah.

And just as He knew how everything was going to come out with Lazarus, He knew what was going to come out in my case. He sees the end from the beginning, according to Isaiah 46:10.

We remember the past, we see the present, but we don't know the future. He does, according to Acts 15:18.

It is our duty to trust Him — and know that He is doing what is best for us. That was the sort of faith that King David showed in Psalm 139 when he wrote: "O Lord, thou hast searched me, and known me. Thou knowest my downsitting and mine uprising.

"Thou understandest my thought afar off. Thou

compassest my path and my lying down, and art ac-
quainted with all my ways.

"For there is not a word in my tongue, but, lo, O
Lord, thou knowest it altogether.

"Thou hast beset me behind and before, and laid
thine hand upon me. Such knowledge is too wonderful for
me; it is high, I cannot attain unto it."

In plain language, David is proclaiming that God
knows everything about us. He knows when we sit and
when we rise. He knows our thoughts, our every move,
and all our ways. Before a word is on your tongue, He
knows what you are going to say. He has his hand upon me
— and you. His ways are so incredible that we cannot
begin to understand them with our human minds.

He sees further than we do. His providence is
perfect. When God delays, it provides a wonderful basis
for trust and praise.

God's delays are loving. Mary and Martha, I think,
questioned the love of the Lord when He did not rush to
Lazarus' bedside and heal him — nor to his deathbed and
raise him up. They did not understand His delay.

Martha even chided Jesus in John 11:21, telling
him, "Lord, if You had been here, my brother would not
have died."

I hate to say this, but at times I felt like chiding the
Lord, too. I felt like saying, "Lord, if You had been here,
I would not be in such pain, I would not be re-learning how
to talk and read and spell all over again." Sometimes, I
questioned whether the Lord really knew where I was.
Maybe He forgot me.

I got a letter from one of our church's missionary
evangelists, Paul Schok, who was doing some evangelism
in Japan. As Violet read it to me, one phrase stuck out from

the rest. He said, "Son, always remember, you can't have a testimony without a test, and Jesus does love you."

I had to learn that it was specifically because Jesus loves me that He allowed me to go through my ordeal. It was because He loved Lazarus and his sisters and the Disciples that He delayed restoring Lazarus.

When Jesus did get to Lazarus' house, He had tender compassion. When Jesus saw their mourning, He was moved deeply, and troubled. "Where have you laid him?" he asked.

"Come see, Lord," they replied.

And there Jesus wept.

Those watching marveled, saying, "See how He loved him?"

They couldn't see into the future, as we can see by their use of the past tense: "See how He loved him?"

Theologian William Barclay once wrote that the ancient Greeks thought that their gods were incapable of responding emotionally. Thus, Jesus demonstrated His humanity to them when "He wept." It literally means He shed tears. God is love, and He loves you in spite of the circumstances in which you find yourself.

I have had to learn that.

God's delays are also precise. Jesus carefully waited until Mary and Martha had buried their brother. When He got there, He knew they had not kept him on ice in expectation of Jesus' tardy arrival. The Master knew it had not occurred to them that He would — or even could — bring their brother back to life.

They had lost their hope of ever seeing him again. They'd had an expectation of Jesus — that He could heal their brother. When that did not happen, they gave up their hope and accepted their brother's death.

Then, Jesus came. When they thought He was not working in their situation, He came. Exactly at His time, He came — not when He was invited.

God's timing is perfect — never a minute too late, never a minute too early. There is a time for everything, declares Ecclesiastes 3:1. He has declared a season for every activity under heaven.

God's delays are purposeful, too. To those He loves and to those who would see His work, His delays serve a great, divine purpose.

I believe that His delay in my sufferings taught me more than I could ever learn otherwise. Through it, I learned enormous compassion for the suffering, how to trust in God, and the power of intercessory prayer.

In short, my experience taught me that when God delays, it is on purpose, never accidental. I learned that when God delays He knows exactly what He is doing — and that when He delays, it is because He loves us.

When God delays it is for a precise time and He ultimately is going to bring more good to you, and more glory to himself.

Would you want it any other way?

I don't think so.

Through the Valley

One day in the summer of 1987, Bob Roberts, one of the board members of Destined to Overcome Ministries, asked if I would like to be the cook on a backpacking trip to the Jefferson Wilderness area in the mighty Cascade Mountains of Oregon.

We loaded up the horses with all of our gear and started down the dusty trail that led us to a picturesque lake at the foot of Three Fingered Jack. The next day Bill, Bob's identical twin brother, and I were to meet Bob at a special lake that was not on the trail. To get to this lake we knew we had to use a compass and work our way through the timber. We also knew that once we got there, the fishing would be well worth the effort.

With our lunch on our backs and compass in hand, we started off for the secret lake, not knowing God was going to take us to His classroom.

Now I have never been lost in the woods; sometimes I get misplaced, but never lost.

This was one of those times.

Big time!

About noon we decided to sit down and eat our lunch and try to figure out where we had taken a wrong turn. Peanut butter sandwiches are not my favorite on-the-side-of-a-hill snack, but it was all we had.

I knew our day was not going well when Billy asked me, "What's to drink?" I didn't plan on getting misplaced. Okay, lost. But there we were with a substance sticking to the roof of our mouths and not having a thing to wash it down.

As I sat there in misery, I looked across the valley and saw a rock with water coming out of it. We took the cup, went over to the rock, placed it under the moss, and let the cup fill with spring water. I have never in my life tasted such satisfying, thirst-quenching water. We had found a spring that would take care of our needs.

Psalm 84:6 says, "Passing through the valley of Baca, they make it a place of springs."

The valley of Baca means weeping. I think it is significant that no one knows where the valley Baca was, just as we don't know when the weeping times will come our way.

Things happen in our lives that rupture the dam, and the tears begin to flow over the flood gates of our emotions. When the doctors told Violet and I that I was to go through major brain surgery, we wept. At the loss of my ability to speak, to read, to write, I wept. When I thought my ministry was over, I wept.

Looking at this verse, I saw some things.

Weeping is not a permanent thing. It says "Passing through." It is not a stationary place but a place of transition.

Psalm 6:6 says, "I am worn out from groanings; all night long I flood my bed with weeping and drench my couch with tears." I don't know how many pillowcases Violet has changed because of the tears. Tears of uncertainty, tears of what if's.

We found ourselves in the valley of Baca. But, we are not abiding in the valley of Baca, we are only passing through. Those who had to pass through the valley of weeping did not leave it as they found it. They made it a spring.

When God allows things to come your way that cause you to weep, He gives you a choice to make. You can either become bitter or better.

I don't know about you, but I don't like to be around a bitter, stagnant person. But, I love to be around a person who is alive and who likes to live. They take the situations that the sovereign God has allowed to come their way, and they let the Lord make them into a spring of living water that people long to drink from.

The valley of Baca was in the east. The person who had a spring in the east was a friend and a helper to those who did not have any water.

Boy, what a picture.

You have been through a valley of Baca.

You wept.

You saw that God was there, and you made that experience a spring.

You turned the weeping time into a spring.

It is common knowledge that people have a fascination with good water. Bottled spring water is a multi-million dollar business. We buy it in the store, on the airplanes, and order it in restaurants.

There are people in the world who are dying of thirst. They need something to quench their thirst with something beside alcohol and wine, lust and loose living. If you have gone through the valley and allowed the Lord to make a spring out of your valley, God will use you to satisfy their thirst.

It is true that God can take our valleys of weeping and turn them into springs, but God requires us to take certain steps.

Psalm 84:4 says, "Blessed are they that dwell in thy house; they will be still praising thee." The word "dwell" means to settle, to marry. We must be married to God's house. By that, I'm not referring to the church building, I'm referring to the principles of God. We are His tabernacle.

We have a good self-image brought about because we have come to grips with who God is and what He is doing in our lives. We have established trust and the principles of praising God. That word "praising" comes from the word "Halal." It means to be clamorously foolish, to rave.

Are you raving about the Lord's presence in your life? It's only when we praise God in the difficult situations — the ones we have no control over — that God begins to make a spring.

Psalm 84:5 says, "Blessed are those whose strength is in you . . ." (NIV). I'm sorry to say that, without realizing it, I trusted in myself more than I trusted in God.

When the sovereign God allowed things to happen in my life that I didn't have any control over, I found out that my trust was in my own abilities, not God's. Today, I have shifted my strength from me to God.

My strength is in You, my hope is in You, my trust is in You, Oh God!

When this principle is in place — that is the time our weeping turns into strengths.

The rest of Psalm 84:5 says, ". . . who have set their hearts on pilgrimage" (NIV). That means they have established God's ways in their hearts. We need to make adjustments from our own ways to the ways of God. In other words, we make a realignment of our hearts. God showed me that faith was a journey, not a destination.

Psalm 84:7 says, "They go from strength to strength, till each appears before God in Zion" (NIV). The dealings of the Lord in our lives are a progression. We don't get them all in one dose.

I thank God that He didn't give my speech back, and my abilities back, all at once. If He had, I think I know myself well enough, I would have had a tendency to revert back to the old Duane Parrish.

He has left the residue as a reminder. I talk with a limp. I mis-pronounce words, and I have to slow down. Every time I do that, I'm jettisoned back to the place where I could only say, "Oh God," and I'm reminded of how good God is.

Psalm 84:10 says, "Better is one day in your courts than a thousand elsewhere; I would rather be a door keeper in the house of my God than dwell in the tents of the wicked." Those people who genuinely love God are the ones who can turn the weeping times into springs.

It is God who gives you the desire, that longing in

your heart to please Him. Our response to that longing is to say, "God I don't care if I'm a Billy Graham or not, I just want to be in Your presence. I will do whatever You want me to do. I want to be Your servant. If it's a doorkeeper in Your house, that's what I want to be."

If all these principles are in place, those who are thirsty will be coming to you for a refreshing, thirst-quenching drink.

Smile, God Is Making a Picture

During my rehabilitation period, I needed something to do with my time besides speech therapy. I needed to relax and get my mind off my problems.

One of the widows in my church offered to teach me how to make stained glass pictures, and I jumped at the chance. I had always admired stained glass, and now I was going to get to learn how to do it. Although, at the time, I could only show her through my expressions, she could tell I was excited about the idea.

Frances Bemmers Ashford was a very patient teacher. I will always be grateful to her for that. Little did I realize during the sessions we would spend together, teacher and pupil, that God was going to begin to unfold some important truths to me.

At each step in the process, the Lord was there to reveal a truth for that particular step. God is after change in our lives. He wants us to keep being transformed into His likeness.

Second Corinthians 3:18 says, "And we, who with unveiled faces all reflect the Lord's glory, are being transformed into his likeness with ever-increasing glory, which comes from the Lord, who is the Spirit" (NIV).

We as Christians can't go through life being the same. God longs to make our lives a picture that is beautiful and admired by those around us, to point us to Christ. Oftentimes, our lives are far from a beautiful picture. There are unclean thoughts that plague us, dishonesty, or sins that are unconfessed.

When you turn to God, in a salvation experience, He comes into your life and saves you from sin — any and all sins. When Christ comes into your life, you have residing in you *all* of Christ.

Christ doesn't come into your life and say, "You have a little of Me; be good, then I will bring more of myself to you."

It is important for you to remember that God won't push you into any change in your life that will make you into the beautiful picture He has for you. God waits to be discovered.

You see, residing in us is:

Forgiveness: Matthew 6:14 says, "For if you forgive men when they sin against you, your heavenly Father will also forgive you" (NIV).

Peace: John 14:27 says, "Peace I leave with you; my peace I give you . . ." (NIV).

Healer: Jeremiah 30:17 says, "But I will restore you to health and heal your wounds, declares the Lord . . ." (NIV).

Truth: John 14:6 says, "Jesus answered, 'I am the way and the truth and the life. No one comes to the Father except through me' " (NIV).

Knowledge: Proverbs 1:7 says, "The fear of the Lord is the beginning of knowledge."

Deliverance: John 8:32 says, "Then you will know the truth and the truth will make you free" (NIV). The Greek word for free means to be liberated, unrestrained, a citizen, not a slave.

It is important to remember that man works on the outside to make us look macho. God, however, works on the inside to make of us a beautiful portrait of the likeness of Christ who is living in our lives.

I chose to do a stained glass image of the dove of the Holy Spirit. While working on my chosen project, God impressed upon me that He knows our lives better than we do. He designs a picture that will reveal Christ to us, and then we can reveal Him to people who have no hope.

These are the steps the Master Artist takes.

1. He sees the picture.

God has a picture for our lives . . . our marriages . . . our fatherhood. It is a picture that will cause people to stand back in awe at how we handle difficult situations.

Romans 8:28-29 says, "And we know that in all things God works for the good of those who love him, who have been called according to his purpose. For those that God foreknew he also predestined to be conformed to the likeness of his son, that he might be the firstborn among many brothers" (NIV).

2. He selects the glass.

Broken glass . . . bright-colored glass . . . dark glass.

3. He puts the pattern on the glass.

We need to pattern our lives after God's Word and not what men say, but what He is saying to us through His Word.

Psalms 119:9-11 says, "How can a young man keep his way pure? By living according to your word. I seek you with all my heart; do not let me stray from your commands. I have hidden your word in my heart that I might not sin against you" (NIV).

When God traces the outline on our hearts, He will test us on what He has traced.

4. He begins to cut the glass.

The glass must be prostrate before the artist.

God wants to develop in us a prayer life. If we are going to have any impact on other lives, we are going to have to be a praying people.

The glass is then cut with a special glass-cutter, which is dipped in oil. That speaks to us of the anointing of God. We have to pray ourselves empty before God can fill us.

Then pressure is put on the glass by the glass cutter, tracing the pattern that now lays on the glass.

Then the glass is held very firm and tapped on very gently with the cutter. All the un-wanted, un-useful, un-needed, un-productive, and un-necessary glass falls off.

James 1:2-4 says, "Consider it pure joy, my brothers, whenever you face trials of many kinds, because you know that the testing of your faith develops perseverance. Perseverance must finish its work so that you may be mature and complete, not lacking anything" (NIV).

5. He grinds off the rough spots.

The artist then takes the pattern and puts it on the new piece to check where the high spots are. Then he takes the piece to the grinder.

The beautiful pieces of stained glass have this one thing in common: they have been placed up against the grinding wheel.

God is perfecting in our lives qualities that will be beautiful if we submit to God's grinder. Every church has a grindstone and also a crank to turn the grindstone. Life itself has its share of grindstones.

6. He darkens the edges.

The glass artist then takes a dark pen and blackens the edge around the piece. Then he wraps the edges in copper foil.

This is done so the dark edging will hide the copper foil and make it blend in with the picture. The darkness represents the trials and testings we go through. The copper foil represents the self-life.

We must understand that God has chosen human vessels to carry His message to the world. We must also realize that we must die to our own self and live unto Him.

John 3:30 says, "He must increase, but I must decrease." That means to lessen in rank or influence; make lower.

7. He then puts the pieces together.

We sometimes feel like our whole life is in pieces, and we cannot be used of God. Bring all your pieces to the Master Artist and say to Him, "Mold me and make me into Your servant."

8. He brushes on the flux and solders the pieces together.

The flux is an acid that raises the dirt and any impurities to the surface so the solder will hold.

When we are in prayer, there is a cleansing that takes place. All our sin is brought to the surface so we can deal with it.

9. He then takes the lead cameing and applies it to the border of the picture.

The lead cameing is a U-shaped lead that forms around the border of the picture to make it complete.

When I cut the lead cameing, it was too short. My teacher saw the look on my face.

She said, "That's all right, we will get the cameing stretcher." I put the lead cameing in the jaws of the stretcher, holding the jaws down with my thumb. Frances got a pair of pliers and grabbed the other end of the cameing. We played a game of tug-of-war and in the end, the piece that was too short was now an inch too long.

We might feel we can't do the ministry that God is laying on our hearts, but He can stretch us.

10. For the last step he puts on the patina.

The patina is a solution you put over the lead to take the shininess away so that people who are looking at the art work are not distracted.

Yielding to the will of God in our testing times changes us into the image of God. Then those looking on will not be distracted by self; instead they will see Jesus in our lives.

I live for those times when, in church, I can look at those people standing before me who have come to the altar, admitting they are going through a trial, that they are going through the fire, and they don't know what to do. I don't have any magic. I don't have any formula that I can say "do this and do that and you will be on your way." All I can do is pour my life into these vessels and say, "Here is what God has done in my life. He's brought me back to happiness. He's brought me back to the purposes in the ministry that He has for me to do, and He can do the same for you."

Violet and I know first-hand that trials and testings can produce heartache, stress, and depression. Our mission is to help those who are suffering to look beyond the moment and consider God's full-blown portrait of their lives. The beauty of the finished masterpiece results — not from ending the trial — but from the new-found, intimate relationship with God — a relationship that can only come through testing.

That's why we can say, "Smile, God is making a picture."

Epilogue

My healing took approximately seven years.

It took that long to reach a place where I was back to normal, or semi-normal. About that time I began to feel the people of Christ Center were becoming tired (and rightly so) of hearing about my surgery and how excited I was about my progress.

I could sense a change coming in my life, but what? I was being asked to speak in different churches and different denominations and share what God had done in my life and was still doing. I couldn't actually fulfill those requests and still be a good pastor. I sought council from highly respected brothers in the ministry whom I regarded as being men of sound wisdom and sound judgment. They had influenced my life again and again, and I thought they could tell me what was going on.

I remember taking them out to dinner, breakfast, lunch, and so on. I painted a picture of what I perceived God was saying to me. He wanted me to leave a secure position and go out in faith and start a ministry telling people that they didn't need to give up because God was there. This idea was in its embryonic stages and I listed all the negatives, hoping my friends would tell me I was crazy to leave such a secure position at my age.

But every one of them said, "God is speaking to your heart. Go for it."

Well, I was filled with fright and fear and all those things. I resigned to my board, they smiled and took my resignation. Two of the board members said, "Pastor, we knew that you were going to resign tonight." I said, "How did you know that?" Each one of them answered, "In prayer last night God spoke to us that we were to take your resignation because He has a new ministry for you."

That's how the ministry started, ever so slowly.

I remember going to Bill Gothard's pastors' meeting in Portland. I didn't know what to call this ministry. I just wanted God to have His say in the matter, so I took it to prayer and said, "God, what do You want me to call this ministry?" When we were exiting a service, going out to the foyer to get some water and some coffee, it was just like a lightning bolt came to me: "Call this ministry, Destined to Overcome." So I went back into the service when it reconvened and I saw a pastor of a large church that is a close brother of mine. I said, "Hey Dick, I have found out what God wants me to call this ministry."

He said, "What's that?"

I replied, "Destined to Overcome Ministries."

He said, "Oh that is a fantastic name for a ministry and it suits you to a tee."

There are still some things that I can't do — things that have hung on after the surgery. I forget what I'm told from one day to the next, or what I said I would do the next day. Violet must proofread everything I write because you never know how I will put a thought that I had in my head down on paper. My spelling is much worse than before surgery. Sometimes I have to have Violet spell for me because even the spell-checker on my computer must have at least the starting of the word to be able to look it up correctly. We have both learned to cope with the inabilities.

In a family that goes through a problem, each one is tested. Each one will respond. Sometimes it will take each member a length of time to respond correctly. My boy Mark had a difficult time at first responding to a loving God who would allow this to happen to his Dad. After going through the Teen Challenge Program he found a new lease on life and a better understanding about the sovereignty of God.

Then there is Patrece, my daughter. She went away to college and met her husband, Patrick McKay. They are now youth pastors in a church in Portland, Oregon. They have three wonderful sons — a set of twins, Bret and Bradley, and a singleton, Brandon. Patrece has gone through counseling since leaving our home and we are building what Satan wanted to tear apart, a relationship that is second to none.

I love my family.

Violet and I have never been so at peace knowing that we are doing the will of God. Wherever we go there are hurting people. They lack knowledge of the sovereignty of God. They desperately need someone who can say simply, "I have been there."

Destined to Overcome Ministries strives to bring this message to churches as well as the individual. In analyzing the burden that God has placed on my heart, four words stand out above all others: compassion, comfort, confrontation, and commitment.

Let me take each word and see if I can explain to you what is in my heart and the feelings that are continually there and what I plan to do as we go further in this ministry.

Compassion. There has never been a time when I share what God has done for us that I don't feel compassion welling up in my spirit. Over and over the Scriptures say, "Jesus was moved by compassion." When God allows me to bring the people and their needs to Him, I find compassion flowing from my heart, and I believe that it's God flowing through my heart to their heart and saying, "Hey, don't give up." At that moment I am closer to the compassion of Christ.

Comfort. One of the benefits derived from compassion is comfort. The look on faces around the altar when people meet with God and hear Him speak, "It is I, be not afraid," is priceless. The transparency with which I share the testimony (and I have nothing to hide)... I seek to share with them the divine side and the human side. It is both embarrassing and painful when I have to say to them, "I thought about committing suicide, I had the gun to my head." That was the human side; I didn't trust the Lord. When I share that transparent self with the people, and when I tell them what God has done in my life, it gives those people hope whereby they receive comfort.

Confrontation. So many people have a hard time coming to grips with their problems. They think, "Where did I fail God?" or, "What is God punishing me for?" They hear conflicting voices in the ultra faith message. Sharing what I have been through, the anger at God, the fear, the loneliness, and being in the depths of depression to the point of self-destruction, has a way of encouraging the believers to trust God in the midst of the storm. I had to confront the attitudes of my life. And you know what? They began to see their need to do the same, to confront those attitudes and bring them to the foot of the Cross and thereby receive the grace that they need for that trial.

Commitment. I have never in all my life been so committed to the ways of Christ. God allowed some things to touch my life. I in turn hope to motivate those who come in contact with Destined to Overcome Ministries, Duane Parrish, Violet Parrish, to be commited to the ways of Christ and thereby experience this same joy that is ours. I'm committed also to the pointing of the Church back to the basics. Back to prayer, back to the sovereign move of the Holy Spirit within our churches. I want to see the young and the old alike glimpse a fresh visitation of the Holy Spirit. The Holy Spirit working in their lives in a cleansing way, in a convicting way, in the way that can make them the vessels that can evangelize the world. The testings that God has allowed me to go through in these last 14 years have produced some incredible desires for me to share what God has done in my life, and I would like to share them with you here:

> To minister to the hurting people in our society, our churches, and the world.

> To see a revival of prayer once again return to our churches.

> To present as living proof the message that God is in the transforming business.

> To show the people that it is not by might, not by power but by My Spirit, says the Lord.

> To lead them back to the basics of what trust in God will produce in the life of the believer.

> To point out to them the positive bless-
> ings of going through a major testing.
> To take the message of encouragement,
> both here and overseas.

Like the apostle Paul, I boast in the marvelous things God has done in my life. As we take this message around the world, God is transforming lives.

In a nutshell, tell yourself this when you are facing trouble and testings:

> God brought me here. By His will I am
> in this difficult place. In that fact I will rest.
> Secondly, He will sustain me here in His love
> and give me grace in this trial to behave as His
> child. Third, He will make this trial a blessing,
> teaching me to learn the lessons He intended me
> to learn, and working in me the grace He intends
> to give.

Jeremiah 29:11 says, "For I know the plans that I have for you . . . plans to prosper you and not to harm, plans to give you hope and a future" (NIV).

And in the end, in His good time, He can bring me out again. How and when, only He knows. Therefore my confessions shall be, I am here by God's appointment, in His care, under His training, for His time.

Duane and Violet Parrish

If you would like to get in touch with the Parrishes you
may contact them through:
Destined to Overcome Ministries
6580 Fairway Ave., S.E.
Salem, OR 97306
(503) 585-3952